About Anarchism

Nicolas Walter

FREEDOM

PM

About Anarchism
Nicolas Walter
All contributions © 2019 the respective authors
This edition © 2019 PM Press
All rights reserved. No part of this book may be transmitted by any
means without permission in writing from the publisher.

ISBN: 978-1-62963-640-5
Library of Congress Control Number: 2018948959

Cover by John Yates / www.stealworks.com
Interior design by briandesign

10 9 8 7 6 5 4 3 2 1

PM Press
PO Box 23912
Oakland, CA 94623
www.pmpress.org

Printed in the USA.

■ Contents

◾ Preface

By David Goodway

About Anarchism appeared originally in June 1969 as the hundredth number of Colin Ward's celebrated *Anarchy*, a periodical to which Nicolas Walter was a frequent contributor. Freedom Press then immediately proceeded to bring it out as a booklet. The rest of its publication history is explained by Natasha Walter in her "Introduction" below. It was translated into many other languages, and it is said that its popularity led some anarchist parents to name their boys "Nicolas". By the way, readers should note the correct spelling of "Nicolas": it regularly appears with an erroneous "h". When my daughter Emma told him one of her names is 'Nicola', he enquired after its spelling, responding instantly, "Yes, that's the best way!"

Something of the considerable influence *About Anarchism* exerted is revealed by Peter Marshall in his autobiography *Bognor Boy: How I Became an Anarchist* (2018). He believes that the key factors in his becoming an anarchist were the events of May 1968 in Paris, together with reading both Wilde's *The Soul of Man under Socialism* and *About Anarchism*.

Nicolas wrote a mass of anarchist journalism, but *About Anarchism* was the most sustained (as well as successful) anarchist publication of his lifetime. *The Anarchist Past* and *Damned Fools in Utopia* are selections from his articles and pamphlets that I edited posthumously in 2007 and 2011 respectively.

About Anarchism continues to read freshly after fifty years. It's succinct, straightforwardly written—even lucid—comprehensive and astonishingly non-sectarian. I warm particularly to the way in which, after distinguishing between philosophical anarchism, individualism and egoism, mutualism and federalism, collectivism and communism, and syndicalism, he observes that these differences have become less important, "more apparent than real" and "artificial differences of emphasis", rather than "serious differences of principle". I doubt this is true, whether in 1969 or 2019, but I wish that it were!

•

Nicolas Hardy Walter was born in 1934, in South London, where his father was researching at the Maudsley Hospital, and was rightly proud of his dissenting family background over several generations. His paternal grandfather, Karl Walter (1880–1965), a journalist, had as a young man been an anarchist, had known Peter Kropotkin and Edward Carpenter, and with Tom Keell was one of the two English delegates to the International Anarchist Congress at Amsterdam in 1907. Three years before he had married Margaret Hardy, an American woman he had met in Italy; and between 1908 and the First World War they lived in the States, where he worked on the *Kansas City Star*. In the 1930s, they settled in Italy, Karl Walter as a sympathizer of fascism; but in old age he returned to both anarchism and London, and in the last years of his life was writing occasionally for *Freedom* at the same time as his grandson. Nicolas's father W. Grey Walter (1910–1977) was a brilliant neurologist who created ingenious electro-mechanical robots, wrote *The Living Brain* (1953)—widely read in its Pelican edition—was Director for many years of the Burden Neurological Institute in Bristol and appeared on television in the BBC's *The Brains Trust*.

Nicolas's maternal grandfather was S.K. (Samuel Kerkham) Ratcliffe (1868–1958), another journalist, who had also known Kropotkin and Carpenter (at whose funeral he was a mourner) and had served on the executive of the Fabian Society alongside Charlotte Wilson (whose anarchist essays his grandson was to edit). Although acting editor of the daily *Statesman* of Calcutta, 1903–1906, and editor of the *Sociological Review*, 1910–1917, he was essentially a freelance journalist—and a rationalist liberal rather than a socialist—but he was also a formidable lecturer, undertaking no fewer than twenty-eight lecture tours of the USA and Canada. He served for forty years as "an appointed lecturer" of the South Place Ethical Society, the history of which he was to write, and Nicolas followed him in this role from 1978.

S.K.'s brother William Ratcliffe became a painter and was a member of the Camden Town Group. Nicolas's mother Monica had been one of Ninette de Valois's dancers at Sadler's Wells. Grey Walter (who was three times married) and Monica Walter divorced when Nicolas was nine or ten, and he was brought up by his mother and her second husband, A.H.W. (Bill) Beck, who was to become Professor of Engineering at Cambridge.

Nicolas was sent to private schools in the Bristol area and then boarded at a minor and semi-progressive public school, Rendcomb College, Cirencester (to which E.D. Morel and John Middleton Murry had sent sons). On leaving school he did his two years' National Service in the RAF as a Junior Technician in Signals Intelligence. He was one of those bright young men who were taught Russian as part of the Cold War effort; and it was on Russia, second only to British history and anarchism, that he was to write most extensively and percipiently—for a considerable period he was contemplating a biography of Kropotkin.

In 1954, he went up to Exeter College, Oxford, to read Modern History. At Oxford he was a member of the Labour Club—he had been "brought up more or less as a Labour Party supporter—an extreme left-wing Labour Party supporter"[1]—but in the autumn of 1956 the twin upheavals of the Suez Crisis and the Hungarian Revolution jolted him to question the accepted ideologies. On graduating in 1957, he left for London where he was to spend his entire working life, initially as a schoolteacher—among his first pupils was Christine Barnett, nine years his junior, who would later become his second wife—but soon moving on to political research, publishing and journalism. He participated in the political and cultural ferment of the first New Left, frequenting the Partisan Coffee House in Carlisle Street, and advocating nuclear disarmament before the actual formation of the Campaign for Nuclear Disarmament (CND) in 1958. Late in 1958, Karl Walter was responsible for introducing him to Lilian Wolfe, who had been Tom Keell's companion and continued to live at Whiteway colony but during the week worked for Freedom Press, then in Red Lion Street. Nicolas began to visit the Freedom Bookshop and to attend the London Anarchist Group's weekly meetings. From 1959, he became a contributor to *Freedom*, an association only terminated by his death.

When in the autumn of 1960 dissatisfaction with CND's legal methods and constitutional agitation spawned within it the direct-action Committee of 100, Nicolas had his first letter published in the *Times* defending the

---

1   Richard Boston, "Conversations about Anarchism", *Anarchy* no. 85 (March 1968): 75.

dissidents, and as a consequence was invited to become a member of the Committee to help round up the well-known names to the all-important figure of one hundred. As he was to write: "I was never at all important in the Committee of 100, but it was very important to me".[2] The Committee of 100 was the leading anarchist—or at least near anarchist—political organization of modern Britain. The events of 1960–1962 led Nicolas to spend as much time as possible during the winter of 1961–1962, outside of work and his considerable political activity, in the Reading Room of the British Museum attempting with considerable success, to work out the historical lineage and above all the political theory of the Committee of 100, in "Damned Fools in Utopia" for the *New Left Review* and especially two *Anarchy* essays, "Direct Action and the New Pacifism" and "Disobedience and the New Pacifism". The *Anarchy* essays won him the greatly valued friendship of Alex Comfort, whom he properly concluded was "the true voice of nuclear disarmament, much more than Bertrand Russell or anyone else" and who was their principal theoretical influence, alongside the novelist Colin MacInnes.[3] For many years he intended to write a history of the Committee of 100, and of all his unrealized books this is the one I most regret.

In June 1961, Nicolas had resigned from the Committee because of disagreement with its rhetoric and tactics, which had worried him from the outset. The failure of the demonstration at the Wethersfield airbase on December 9 led the following year to the decentralization of the Committee into thirteen regional Committees (several of which were already existent). Although there

---

2   Nicolas Walter, *Damned Fools in Utopia: And Other Writings on Anarchism and War Resistance*, David Goodway, ed. (Oakland, CA: PM Press, 2011), 5.

3   The description of Comfort appears in "Disobedience and the New Pacifism", *Anarchy* no. 14 (April 1962): 112.

was a nominal National Committee of 100, the dominant body now became the London Committee of 100,
which Nicolas joined at its inaugural meeting in April
1962. Another member was the twenty-year-old Ruth
Oppenheim, a microbiologist at Sainsbury's, who also
worked whenever she could in the Committee's Goodwin
Street premises. Barbara Smoker remembers that at the
meetings Nicolas and Ruth always sat together at the
front—and in September they married.

The long, harsh winter of 1962–1963, one of the century's worst, saw renewed crisis, now acted out in the
London Committee. The radicals, mainly from or close
to *Solidarity*, circulated the arrestingly titled discussion
document *Beyond Counting Arses*, advocating radical, subversive action: "We must attempt to hinder the warfare
state in every possible way".[4] It was essentially this group,
joined by Nicolas and Ruth, that constituted the Spies
for Peace, locating and breaking into the Regional Seat
of Government at Warren Row, producing the pamphlet
Danger! Official Secret: RSG-6 and, thereby, diverting many of
us on the Aldermaston March of Easter 1963 to explore the
sinister surface buildings of the subterranean bunker. The
disclosure of the preparations to rule the country through
fourteen RSGs in the event of nuclear war represented,
of course, "a substantial breach of official secrecy" and
caused, as one had assumed, Harold Macmillan's minis-
try real concern.[5] Nicolas, the only member of the Spies
for Peace ever to have declared himself publicly, did so
unambiguously as early as 1968, remarkably, and on the
radio at that—his account of 1973 in *Inside Story*, "The Spies
for Peace Story", was unattributed and continued to be

---

4   *Solidarity* 2, no. 11 (1963) reprinted the text of *Beyond Counting Arses*. The
     sentence quoted appears on page 12.
5   Peter Hennessy, *The Secret State: Whitehall and the Cold War* (London: Allen
     Lane-Penguin Books, 2002), 101 ff., 169.

so in 1988 in "The Spies for Peace and After" (reprinted in *Damned Fools in Utopia*).

At the time of the Spies of Peace Ruth was pregnant with their first child, Susannah; and a second daughter, Natasha, followed shortly. Considerably influenced by her increasingly proud father, Natasha Walter is now a prominent literary journalist and author. In 1963, he became Deputy Editor of *Which?* and a staff writer for the *Good Food Guide*, and from 1965 Press Officer for the British Standards Institution. It was while working for the British Standards Institution that he underwent his only period of imprisonment. The Labour Party Conference was held in Brighton in 1966, as the Vietnam War grew in intensity, as did the Labour government's complicity, and the Vietnam Action Group planned to disrupt the traditional pre-conference service at the Dorset Road Methodist Church. Demonstrators were issued with admission tickets forged by Pat Pottle and Terry Chandler's Stanhope Press. Terry thought it a good idea to print more tickets than had been asked for, and Nicolas was among those he let have one. So it was that Nicolas initiated cries of "Hypocrite!" too early, while George Brown, the deputy prime minister, was speaking, and when Harold Wilson mounted the pulpit to read the second lesson "pandemonium broke loose". Nicolas and Jim Radford were charged with indecent behaviour in church under the Ecclesiastical Courts Jurisdiction Act, 1866, and each sentenced to two months in Brixton. Nothing was to give Nicolas more satisfaction than to read in Wilson's memoirs the admission that this was "one of the most unpleasant experiences of my premiership".[6]

---

6   Harold Wilson, *The Labour Government, 1964–1970: A Personal Record* (London: Weidenfeld and Nicolson and Michael Joseph, 1971), 288.

In 1968, he became chief sub-editor of the *Times Literary Supplement* (TLS), under the admired editorship of Arthur Crook, who made a series of impressive appointments. This was a job for which Nicolas was ideally suited and which he relished. He did not, however, approve of the TLS changing from anonymous to signed reviews and so moved to the Rationalist Press Association (RPA), first as editor of the *New Humanist*, from 1975 to 1985, and then as Director of the RPA until his retirement at the end of 1999. Work at the RPA enabled him to be paid for propagating the dual cause of atheism and rationalism—together with anarchism, the passions of his intellectual life—and this in part by writing letters to the press.

This latter was the capacity in which Nicolas was known to the wider public. It was estimated in 1994 that he had written fourteen thousand letters to newspapers and periodicals with a success rate of some two thousand published (or one or two a week). These appeared not only under his own name but under a variety of pseudonyms: Arthur Freeman, Anna Freeman, Mary Lewis, Jean Raison and others. ("MH" in *Freedom* was originally the abbreviation for the collaborative "Many Hands", but was later used by Nicolas exclusively.) This enormous body of letters, frequently correcting trivial errors, gave the impression of a pernickety and pedantic obsessive; and on retiring as editor of the *Spectator*, Charles Moore included Nicolas in the select group of bores whom he certainly would not miss. The astringency of his extensive book reviewing, from *Freedom* to the *London Review of Books*, contributed to an erroneous public persona of a desiccated and negative crank. The man in reality was the exact reverse: warm, generous, humorous, loved by children, a wonderful friend.

In the 1960s alone, Nicolas had had several contracts from commercial publishers, advances were paid, but the books were never written and the advances were refunded—even though his young family could have done with the money. It was a mystery to admirers such as myself why he did not produce the books that his great gifts and immense energy amply equipped him for. The explanation seems to lie in his perfectionism: he completed innumerable articles to his personal satisfaction, yet he was unable to do this at book-length. The contract that resulted in *Anarchy in Action* was passed on from Nicolas to Colin Ward, but Colin here—and even more in other books—incorporated and built on existing work; Paul Goodman, Alex Comfort and George Woodcock were also obvious exemplars of those who were highly successful in recycling already published material.

During the first half of the 1970s Nicolas was drawn into working on Wynford Hicks's attractive papers *Inside Story* and *Wildcat*; collaboration was something he particularly enjoyed and was good at, for he was a social and sociable person. It was in 1983 that he first came into contact with the German anarchist historian Heiner Becker, and by the end of the decade such was their rapport that all Nicolas's scholarly output on anarchist and historical subjects was in effect jointly written with Heiner. When Peter Marshall and myself withdrew (presciently as matters worked out) from involvement in Freedom Press's projected new quarterly publication, Heiner stepped in, conceived the *Raven*, and in association with Nicolas brought out a run of seven outstanding issues (1987–1989).

In 1974, Nicolas had been diagnosed as having testicular cancer. One testicle was extracted, he was treated with radiotherapy and for a while all seemed fine. Then he began to have problems with his digestive system, he constantly vomited and his weight plummeted from twelve to eight stone [168 to 112 pounds]. It was eventually realized that excessive doses of radiation had damaged the adjoining area of his body. A considerable length of intestine was removed, and he began to recover his health. In 1983, however, it became apparent that his spine and the upper muscles of his thighs had also been affected and progressive disablement set in. As he announced in a letter to the *Guardian*:

> I contracted cancer in my thirties, began to suffer from the long-term side-effects of radiotherapy in my forties, and am now suffering from progressive paralysis and other complications in my fifties.[7]

First he had to use crutches, but by 1997 this formerly fit and very vigorous man was confined to a wheelchair. When asked in 1994 why he did not sue the NHS, he retorted:

> Why should I? It was just bloody bad luck. I'm not complaining. I have only got praise for the people working in hospitals and the social services, even though they are all exhausted and the hospitals are filthy. If I sued the NHS for negligence and won, it would mean there was less money for other people.[8]

Ruth and Nicolas had divorced in 1982. He had the good sense and great fortune to marry Christine Morris (née Barnett), like Ruth Oppenheim a secular Jew, in 1987. Their way of life was to live during the week in the flat on the top storey of 88 Islington High Street above the RPA offices, where Christine also worked for five years, and to spend weekends at her house in Leighton Buzzard. At the end of 1999, Nicolas retired, Christine

---

7   *Guardian*, September 16, 1993.
8   Hunter Davies, "O Come All Ye Faithless", *Independent*, December 20, 1994.

took redundancy from Relate and they withdrew to live full-time in Leighton Buzzard, from where Nicolas would be able to take the train to St Pancras and work in the new British Library. At just this time, though, the cancer returned; squamous cell carcinoma was diagnosed, and at the beginning of 2000 pronounced terminal. This prognosis he confronted with the fortitude that had characterized his entire life; and in March he was to die at the age of sixty-five.

David Goodway
March 2019

■ Introduction to the 2002 Edition

by Natasha Walter

About Anarchism: **Why Now?**

Anybody who has observed or participated in any recent protest against global inequality can testify that an energetic social movement has surfaced over the last few years. Yet to some people, this movement has one particularly negative side. After protests in Gothenburg during the European Union summit in 2001, the British prime minister termed the protesters an "anarchist travelling circus" and poured scorn on their methods and dreams.

As I walked through the crowds on another protest in London later in 2001, I saw that one group of people was carrying a black banner with red writing on it. "Anarchist travelling circus" read the flag. It certainly wasn't the first time that anarchists have used the words of their enemies as a label of pride, and this time it looked like a particularly neat joke.

But anarchism is often seen only as a joke, and even many of its sympathisers seem to have real problems taking it seriously. Anarchists in the current movement are blamed for its most violent or chaotic moments, even by their friends. Certainly, anarchism can just be a sudden protest, a shout of "No!", a clenched fist, a raised banner, but any dissent worth its salt does not just entail a momentary disruption of everyday life. It also attempts to transform everyday life, day to day.

Nicolas Walter always attempted to communicate the positive aspects of anarchism. He saw anarchism as a realistic way of transforming people's lives, and with its emphasis on the pragmatic elements of anarchist thought, *About Anarchism* sets up many resonances for the contemporary movement against global capitalism.

Ever since the collapse of the experiment in state communism, many experts have concluded that there really is no alternative to the existing way of organising society, but anarchists have never stopped believing in an alternative. Immediately [after] the Russian Revolution took place, anarchists dissented from its authoritarian character, and they are still demanding the freedom that state communism denied, as well as the equality that global capitalism denies.

Anarchism is the one current of political thought that yokes freedom and equality. So anarchists differ from socialists, who put the emphasis on equality, and liberals, who put the emphasis on freedom, because anarchists see that freedom and equality are, in practice, the same thing. Even though many of its participants wouldn't use the label anarchist, this insight that freedom and equality are indivisible is the characteristic insight of the current movement against global inequality, whose members use anti-authoritarian methods, working without hierarchies or leaders to build up their protests, and whose demands are both for a more equitable economic system and for greater freedom for every member of society.

That's not to say that this movement is necessarily anarchist, through and through. Those people who are looking to win freedom and equality today tend not to take the state as their primary target, as most anarchists did in the past. Instead they see capitalism, especially as embodied in the multinational corporation, as the target. This emphasis on the corporation as the great enemy has led some of the most prominent spokespeople for the current resistance movement to argue that the state, in contrast to the corporation, must be benign, since they believe it is the state, and only the state, that can reign back the corporation's most malign effects on individuals' lives. Many writers who support the antiglobalisation movement have argued that the best way forward is for governments to pass laws to reform corporations' behaviour and for more international regulation of global trade by groups of states acting together. They argue, in fact, that the way forward is for the state to take back the power it has ceded to the corporation.

Certainly, governments have often managed to limit the power of corporations—states have instituted minimum wage legislation, outlawed child labour, ensured health and safety standards and so on, and even anarchists are able to see that a state can have benign functions. As Walter says, "we have the liberatory state and the welfare state, the state working for freedom and the state working for equality". But, he adds, "The essential function of the state is to maintain the existing inequality".

This last statement might give those people in the current resistance movement who put all their faith in the state pause for thought. What are governments for? Can they be pushed to bring about equality and freedom, or will they protect equality and freedom only so far as those rights do not conflict with wealth and power, and no further?

Look at the behaviour of our own governments [in the West], who announce their intentions to forgive Third World debt and then encourage arms sales to developing countries, financed by more debt; who announce the benefits of free trade and then hold on to tariffs and subsidies that protect domestic corporations. These apparent contradictions are hardly surprising if the anarchist analysis of the state is correct; that the protection of existing inequality provides that state's very reason to exist.

In this way *About Anarchism* offers a useful critique of some of the arguments that are often heard from the anti-globalisation movement. Nicolas Walter does not argue that those who work for reform of government institutions are misguided, because his pragmatism leads him to understand that it is often the only route forward, but he does argue that to bring about freedom and equality more than reform of the state will be necessary.

And in this way his thought chimes in with much of what is being heard from activists, because although those who have only read the literature of the antiglobalisation movement will often find arguments in favour of state power, those who have actually listened to antiglobalisation activists on the street will hear a thoroughgoing scepticism about the behaviour of governments. It is not a coincidence that the rise of [this] new political activism has occurred at the same time as a decline in voting and a cynicism, especially among the young, about the promises of the state. The reason why people have taken to the streets and to organising in non-governmental organisations, rather than lobbying their MPs and organising for parliamentary elections, is because they feel that the conventional political process will not bring them what they desire.

But if governments will not act, who will? The tradition that Nicolas Walter draws on in *About Anarchism*—the tradition of anarchists from William Godwin to Peter Kropotkin, Emma Goldman to Flores Magon—is another narrative of possible action, of individuals or groups acting without reference to outside authority.

This is the kernel of anarchism. As Walter says, the essence of anarchism, the thing without which it is not anarchism, is the negation of authority over anyone by anyone. This negation of authority is a tough concept to get one's head around right now. Most people have utterly lost faith in the idea that anyone can achieve anything without the support either of the state or of the corporation, without either institutional power or the power created by the market.

The inability to see beyond these agencies has infected all aspects of political debate. Look, for instance, away from the antiglobalisation movement and to the current debate about social policy, which is always now posted as a conflict between public and private provision. Yet anarchists might say that in its present guise, this would be better phrased as a conflict between state and corporation, since the truly public sphere, the sphere that is controlled not by the government but by the people, never gets a look in.

There is another way to envisage a welfare society in which ordinary people do not only work in hospitals and schools but also organise them. Many anarchists have emphasised the idea of mutualism—that the desire for cooperation is as basic a human drive as the desire for authority. But with the rise of state welfare in the early twentieth century, all the old traditions of mutualism that already existed in a country like Britain—the cooperative societies, the community hospitals, the insurance societies—were discredited. Perhaps now, if both state and corporate provision are looking unsatisfactory in their own ways, it is time not just to try out ever more complex amalgams of the two but also to reconsider what Peter Kropotkin called *Mutual Aid*—the principle that people can organise to provide their own welfare.

Another way in which this booklet provides an interesting contribution to the current debates lies in Nicolas Walter's optimistic synthesis of various types of anarchist and socialist and libertarian action. He allows for difference, but because he has such a pragmatic and straightforward view of anarchism, he is also good at picking out what unites all the different strands of anarchist thought and action and how each strand can weave into each other rather than pull apart.

That is particularly useful in the current situation. What we are looking at in the movement for global equality is clearly not a united movement. It would be absurd to pretend that the Zapatista National Liberation Army, which mobilised to fight for the rights of indigenous people in Mexico, and Reclaim the Streets, which organises day-long street parties, were similar organisations. It would be nonsensical to suggest that a self-reliant community in England, like the cooperative at Tinker's Bubble in Somerset, and the movement to take over land by the landless in Brazil, used identical strategies.

And yet there are also obviously strands of thinking that now cross boundaries. Many of the most apparently diverse people and organisations share certain basic goals. They can unite around their commitment to anti-authoritarianism; around their belief that people do act for reasons other than the will to power or the desire for profit; around their desire to see economic organisation based on cooperation and social organisation based on mutual aid; and around their faith in non-violent direct action as a means to bring about a new society. All these ideas are characteristic of these new organisations and have been characteristic of anarchists for more than a century.

Nicolas Walter's approach to difference is honest but also peculiarly inclusive. He sees links between those who use the label anarchist and those who do not, but who embody the anarchist temperament. He sees links between different kinds of anarchist thought. And he sees links between all the different types of action—from propaganda by word and deed to direct action. His ability to see diversity as a series of links rather than a series of fissures may be over-optimistic, but it may also help us to see that, sometimes, what pulls people together is more important than what drives them apart. One of the most hopeful sentences of this hope-filled booklet is this one. "In practice most disputes between reformist and revolutionary anarchists are meaningless, for only the wildest revolutionary refuses to welcome reforms and only the mildest reformist refuses to welcome revolutions, and all revolutionaries know that their work will generally lead to no more than reform, and all reformists know that their work is generally leading to some kind of revolution."

About Nicolas Walter

About Anarchism was written in 1968. Nicolas Walter's second daughter, myself, was born the previous year. Night after night, Nicolas sat at the kitchen table in a little house in an ugly, nondescript suburb of north London. With one foot and then the other, he rocked the pram back and forth, back and forth, with his grumbly baby inside it. At the same time he wrote—in his huge, looping handwriting, in black fountain pen—the first draft of the booklet, which was first published in 1969 as a special edition of the magazine *Anarchy*.

About Anarchism was a labour of love and the fruit of long study of the anarchist movement. Nicolas was startled when it was not only immediately reprinted as a pamphlet by Freedom Press, going through five editions by 1977, but was also translated into many languages, including Japanese, Serbo-Croat, Greek, German, Chinese, Polish and Russian, and developed a reputation in many places, not just among European and North American activists.

After it fell out of print for the last time, in the early eighties, fellow anarchists at Freedom Press wanted to reprint the booklet, but Nicolas resisted. He always insisted that he needed to revise the text before it was reprinted and said that he would add sections on feminism and environmentalism, the most important new directions in the ideology of dissent. These could have been powerful additions. Nicolas had found both challenge and inspiration in the growth of feminist movement. And although he was an urban man through and through, he had an unforced disdain for mere consumerism and a deep connection with the beauty of the countryside. Could this have impelled him to write something valuable about how a more cooperative society might have a kinder relationship with the environment? But these revisions, although they were started, were never completed, and this is the first reprint of this classic work since 1980.

That means that *About Anarchism*, for all its contemporary relevance, is very much a work of its times, shot through with all the idealism of the Sixties. "In the Sixties I did think that everything could be changed for the better", Nicolas told an interviewer from *The Independent* in the Nineties.

Indeed, *About Anarchism* was born out of a lifetime's commitment not just to anarchist ideas but also to action. Five years before he wrote *About Anarchism* Nicolas had made a stab at trying to pull Britain away from the road of authoritarianism and militarism on which it seemed set. In 1962, Nicolas, his wife Ruth and six of their friends, all active in the peace movement, had become frustrated with the direction of contemporary protests. Mass marches and illegal sit-downs were all very well and led to high-profile press reports and many arrests, but what real effect were they having on the growing militarism of the government?

Nicolas and his friends started looking for a way to challenge the power of the state more directly, and over the course of months they debated various ideas. Then one of them remembered that a friend of a friend had once mentioned working at a "secret bunker" near Reading. On the off-chance that they could find out what that secret bunker was all about, he and three others set off for Reading in February 1963.

They drove for hours over ice-covered roads and tramped for hours over snow-covered fields, without having much idea what they were looking for. It was a long shot, an absurd idea, really, but it bore fruit. At the east end of a village called Warren Row, they found a fenced off hill with a padlocked wooden gate and an unmarked hut. They climbed over the gates to find a brick boiler house and a wide concrete ramp leading into the hillside. Wireless aerials stood a little way off, their cables leading into the hill. One of them tried the doors of the boiler house and found them unlocked. They piled in. Another door inside was also unlocked, and swung open to reveal a steep staircase leading into an underground office complex. They ran down the stairs, their feet clattering in the silence, and snatched what papers they could from the desks. Then they rushed out again and drove away.

Examination of the papers showed the group that they had stumbled on a grand secret. They had walked straight into a secret government headquarters called the Regional Seat of Government (RSG) Number 6, built to house government officials in the event of nuclear war. At the time, the British public were being kept entirely in the dark about the plans its own government was making for the survival not of the ordinary people but of a political elite.

Nicolas and his friends, who now called themselves the Spies for Peace, were in possession of a secret that they hoped could change the secret militarism of the government. First of all, four members of the group returned to Warren Row in order to find out more about the secret headquarters. They went there on a Saturday and arrived after midnight. This time, the boiler house door was locked. Standing there in the freezing dark, they carefully picked it, and spent several hours in the installation. Each took on a different task. One took photographs. One copied documents. One traced maps. One ransacked every room, going through every drawer and every cabinet. Then they left with a suitcase full of copied papers and a camera full of photographs.

The group then typed up and duplicated three thousand leaflets explaining what they had found. In the days before the internet or desktop computers, this posed surprising problems of resources and organisation. Secrecy was paramount. They stuffed envelopes with their leaflets in the night, wearing gloves, posted them from post boxes all over London, burnt all their own documents, posted the original photographs to sympathisers and threw the typewriter that they had used into a river. As Nicolas wrote twenty-five years after the event, on the night of Wednesday April 10, 1963, "A secret had escaped, and so had the Spies for Peace".

Telling it now, it sounds rather like a game, but to those eight individuals it meant rather more. All young, all with their lives ahead of them, they were running the risk of long prison sentences for doing what they believed to be right. The immediate effect was explosive. Those thousands of leaflets were posted to newspaper offices and to the houses of celebrities, MPs and protestors, and although the government had slapped a D-notice on any disclosure of the RSG system,[1] the newspapers decided to ignore that warning. By that Saturday the story was splashed over every national newspaper. Thousands of protesters, who were moving through the area on yet another

---

1   An official request to news media editors not to publish or broadcast items on specified subjects for reasons of national security. The system is still in use in the United Kingdom, but is now called a DSMA-Notice (Defence and Security Media Advisory Notice). [editor]

Aldermaston March, immediately came to demonstrate at Warren Row. That day, April 13, also happened to be Ruth Walter's twenty-first birthday. She sat outside Warren Row with Nicolas, drinking cheap red wine in the thin spring sunshine, singing "We Shall Overcome" with the rest of the crowd. "It was the most magical day", she said later, "We suddenly realised that we had got away with it".

Most people seemed to believe that only an insider could have leaked such sensitive and unsettling information. The *Sunday Telegraph* was sure of it, and wrote on April 21: "It would not be surprising if investigation does not bring to light a shrewd political mind directing this brilliant subversive operation", and, on May 19, they wrote about "a mastermind behind the Spies for Peace", a "Jekyll and Hyde character" who was thought to be "a brilliant man who may be doing an important job". Despite—or because of—such feverish speculation, the real spies were never caught or imprisoned.

What did the Spies for Peace achieve in the long term? In a way, very little—the government remained set on its belief that it could fight and survive nuclear war, and the action of the Spies for Peace did not snowball into mass revolutionary activity, as some of them had certainly hoped. In a way, an enormous amount— the idea that people should be informed about the secret military preparations of their government found fertile ground in a changing society. Together with the duplicity exposed by the Profumo case later in the year,[2] the story helped to break down the unquestioning respect that had

---

2   A British political scandal that originated with a brief sexual relationship in 1961 between John Profumo, the Secretary of State for War in Harold Macmillan's Conservative government, and Christine Keeler, a nineteen-year-old would-be model. It contributed to the resignation of Macmillam in 1963 and the defeat of the Conservative government at the 1964 general election.

characterised the British people's relationship with their government. The individual spies were both heartened and dismayed by this mixture of success and failure. As the years went by, Nicolas experienced the characteristic loss of illusion of revolutionaries and understood that, although he may have helped society to change, the future he had once believed in wasn't going to arrive—at least not in his lifetime.

But for Nicolas, the loss of belief in a revolutionary future only surfaced occasionally. Most of the time he went on as he always had done, fiercely protesting against government secrecy, against militarism, for free speech and for peace. Only once was he actually imprisoned. In October 1966, he had taken part in a protest against Britain's policy on the Vietnam War by interrupting a church service in Brighton where Harold Wilson read a lesson. "Hypocrite!" he shouted, "How can you use the word of God to justify your policies?" In 1967, just after I was born, he was sentenced to two months in prison for his role in the protest. I still have the photograph, printed on the front page of the *Sun* (in the days when the *Sun* was a serious newspaper), of the four of us—my parents, my sister and myself at six months—looking quizzically into the camera, just before he was jailed.

Many anarchists are drawn to anarchism because of their personal rebelliousness. And Nicolas was no exception. He was a natural anarchist, with a low tolerance for authority and great reserves of anger. Sent to boarding school as a child, then straight from school to National Service, then straight to Oxford University, he learnt to distrust authority despite—or because of—this traditional background. But, oddly, his own family traditions included anarchism. Karl Walter, his grandfather, was one of two British delegates to the first International Anarchist Congress in Amsterdam in 1907.

Although Nicolas gave up much of his protest activity in his last years, partly because of growing physical disability, he never stopped writing for the anarchist press and speaking at anarchist gatherings. A pamphlet he published in 1986 about the significance of May Day has been credited with inspiring the revival of the First of May as a popular day of protest for anarchists in Britain; and his edition of essays by Charlotte Wilson, an anarchist who helped to found *Freedom*, was even published after his death in 2000. He was interested in the way that a new generation was laying hold of anarchist ideas—although their lack of historical awareness and the absence of a concrete goals for the future often infuriated him. It is sad that he didn't live to see this reprint of his own early work, but his words live on, and in this booklet his voice sounds as those who knew him remember it—fierce and uncompromising, but with a great hopefulness and humanity always flickering away in the background.

Natasha Walter
April 2002

■ Note on the 2002 Edition

This is a new edition of *About Anarchism*, based on the text published in 1969 by Freedom Press, and including previously unpublished revisions which Nicolas Walter prepared in the 1980s, which were kept by Heiner Becker. Thanks are also due to Christine Walter, Ruth Walter and Colin Ward.

■ Introduction

The modern anarchist movement is now a hundred years old, counting from when the Bakuninists entered the First International, and in this country there has been a continuous anarchist movement for ninety years (the Freedom Press has been going since 1886). Such a past is a source of strength, but it is also a source of weakness— especially in the printed world. The anarchist literature of the past weighs heavily on the present and makes it hard for us to produce a new literature for the future. And yet, though the works of our predecessors are numerous, most of them are out of print, and the rest are mostly out of date; moreover, the great majority of anarchist works published in English have been translations from other languages.

This means there is little that we can call our own. What follows is an attempt to add to it by making a fresh statement of anarchism. Such a statement is necessarily an individual view, for one of the essential features of anarchism is that it relies on individual judgement; but it is intended to take account of the general views prevailing in the anarchist movement and to interpret them without prejudice. It is expressed in simple language and without constant reference to other writers or to past events, so that it can be understood without difficulty and without any previous knowledge. But it is derived from what other people have said in the past and does not purport to be original. Nor is it meant to be definitive; there is far more to say about anarchism than can be fitted into these pages, and this summary will no doubt soon be superseded like nearly all that have preceded it.

Above all, I make no claim to authority, for another essential feature of anarchism is that it rejects the authority of any spokesperson. If my readers have no criticism to make, I have failed. What follows is simply a personal account of anarchism drawn from the experience of fifteen years reading anarchist literature and discussing anarchist ideas, and of ten years taking part in anarchist activities and writing in the anarchist press.

May 1969

■ What Anarchists Believe

The first anarchists were people in the English and French revolutions of the seventeenth and eighteenth centuries who were given the name as an insult to suggest that they wanted anarchy in the sense of chaos or confusion. But from the 1840s, anarchists were people who accepted the name as a sign to show that they wanted anarchy in the sense of absence of government. The Greek word *anarkhia*, like the English word "anarchy", has both meanings; people who are not anarchists take them to come to the same thing, but anarchists insist on keeping them apart. For more than a century, anarchists have been people who believe not only that absence of government need not mean chaos and confusion, but that a society without government will actually be better than the society we live in now.

Anarchism is the political elaboration of the psychological reaction against authority which appears in all human groups. Everyone knows the natural anarchists who will not believe or do something just because someone tells them to, and everyone can imagine circumstances in which virtually everyone will disagree or disobey. Throughout history the practical tendency towards anarchy is seen among individuals and groups rebelling against those who rule them. The theoretical idea of anarchy is also very old; thus, the description of a past golden age without government may be found in the thought of ancient China and India, Egypt and Mesopotamia, and Greece and Rome, and in the same way the wish for a future utopia without government may be found in the thought of countless religious and political writers and communities. But the application of anarchy to the present situation is more recent, and it is only in the anarchist movement of the nineteenth century that we find the demand for a society without government here and now.

Other groups on both left and right want to get rid of government in theory, either when the market is so free that it needs no more supervision or when the people are so equal that they need no more restraint, but the measures they take seem to make government stronger and stronger. It is the anarchists, and the anarchists alone, who want to get rid of government in practice. This does not mean that anarchists think all human beings are naturally good or identical or perfectible or any romantic nonsense of that kind. It means that anarchists think almost all human beings are sociable and similar and capable of living their own lives and helping each other. Many people say that government is harmful, because no one can be trusted to look after anyone else. If all people are so bad that they need to be ruled by others, anarchists ask, how can anyone be good enough to rule others? Power tends to corrupt, and absolute power corrupts absolutely. At the same time the wealth of the earth is the product of the labour of human-ity as a whole, and every human being has an equal right to take part in continuing the labour and enjoying the product. Anarchism is an ideal type which demands at the same time total freedom and total equality.

Liberalism and Socialism

Anarchism may be seen as a development from either liber-alism or socialism, or from both liberalism and socialism.

Like liberals, anarchists want freedom; like socialists, anarchists want equality. But we are not satisfied by liberalism alone or by socialism alone. Freedom without equality means that the poor and weak are less free than the rich and strong, and equality without freedom means that we are all slaves together. Freedom and equality are not contradictory but complementary; in place of the old polarisation of freedom versus equality—according to which we are told that more freedom equals less equality and more equality equals less freedom—anarchists point out that in practice you cannot have one without the other. Freedom is not genuine if some people are too poor or too weak to enjoy it, and equality is not genuine if some people are ruled by others. The crucial contribution to political theory made by anarchists is this realisation that freedom and equality are in practice the same thing.

Anarchism also departs from both liberalism and socialism in taking a different view of progress. Liberals see history as a linear development from savagery, superstition, intolerance and tyranny to civilisation, enlightenment, tolerance and emancipation. There are advances and retreats, but the true progress of humanity is from a bad past to a good future. Socialists see history as a dialectical development from savagery through despotism, feudalism and capitalism to the triumph of the proletariat and the abolition of the class system. There are revolutions and reactions, but the true progress of humanity is again from a bad past to a good future.

Anarchists see progress quite differently, in fact they often do not see progress at all. We see history not as a linear or a dialectical development in one direction but as a dualistic process. The history of all human society is the story of a struggle between the rulers and the ruled, between the haves and the have-nots, between the people who want to govern and be governed and the people want to free themselves and their fellows; the principles of authority and liberty, of government and rebellion, of state and society, are in perpetual opposition. This tension is never resolved; the movement of human society in general or of a particular human society is now in one direction now in another. The rise of a new regime or the fall of an old one is not a mysterious break in development or an even more mysterious part of development but is exactly what it seems to be. Historic events are welcome only to the extent that they increase freedom and equality for the whole people; there is no hidden reason for calling a bad thing good because it is inevitable. We cannot make any useful predictions of the future, and we cannot be sure that the world is going to get better. Our only hope is that, as knowledge and consciousness increase, people will become more aware that they can live their own lives without any need for authority.

Nevertheless, anarchism does derive from liberalism and socialism both historically and ideologically. Liberalism and socialism came before anarchism, and anarchism arose from their complementarities and contradictions; most anarchists still begin as either liberals or socialists, or both. The spirit of revolt is seldom born fully grown, and it generally grows into rather than within anarchism. In a sense, anarchists always remain liberals and socialists, and whenever they reject what is good in either they betray anarchism itself. On one hand, we depend on freedom of speech, assembly, movement, behaviour, and especially on the freedom to differ; on the other hand, we depend on equality of possessions, on human solidarity, on the practice of mutual aid, and especially on the sharing of power. We are liberals but more so and socialists but more so.

Yet anarchism is not just a mixture of liberalism and socialism; that is social democracy or welfare capitalism, the system which prevails in this country.[1] Whatever we owe to and however close we are to liberals and socialists, we differ fundamentally from them—and from social democrats—in rejecting the institution of government. Both liberals and socialists depend on government—liberals ostensibly to preserve freedom but actually to prevent equality, socialists ostensibly to preserve equality but actually to prevent freedom. Even the most extreme liberals and socialists cannot do without government, the exercise of authority by some people over other people. The essence of anarchism, the one thing without which it is not anarchism, is the negation of authority over anyone by anyone.

Democracy and Representation

Many people oppose undemocratic government, but anarchists differ from them in also opposing democratic government. Some people oppose democratic government as well, but anarchists differ from them in doing so not because they fear or hate the rule of the people, but because they believe that democracy is not the rule of the people—that democracy is in fact a logical contradiction, a physical impossibility. Genuine democracy is possible only in a small community where everyone can take part in every decision; and then it is not necessary. What is called democracy and is alleged to be the government of the people by the people for the people is in fact the government of the people by elected rulers and would be better called "consenting oligarchy".

Government by rulers whom we have chosen is different from and generally better than government by rulers who have chosen themselves, but it is still government of some people by other people. Even the most democratic

---

1   Here the author refers to the UK in the 1980s. [editor]

government still depends on someone making someone else do something or stopping someone else doing something. Even when we are governed by our representatives we are still governed, and as soon as they begin to govern us against our will they cease to be our representatives. Most people now agree that we have no obligation to a government which we have not chosen; anarchists go further and insist that we have no obligation to a government we have chosen. We may obey it because we agree with it, or because we are too weak to disobey it, but we have no obligation to obey it when we disagree with it and are strong enough to disobey it. Most people now agree that those who are involved in any change should be consulted about it before any decision is made; anarchists go further and insist that they should themselves make the decision and go on to put it into effect.

So anarchists reject the idea of a social contract and the idea of representation. In practice, no doubt, most things will always be done by a few people—by those who are interested in a problem and are capable of solving it—but there is no need for them to be selected or elected. They will always emerge anyway, and it is better for them to do so naturally. The point is that leaders and experts do not have to be rulers, that leadership and expertise are not necessarily connected with authority. And when representation is convenient, that is all it is. The only true representatives are the delegates or the deputies who are mandated by those who send them and who are subject to instant recall by them. In some ways the ruler who claims to be a representative is worse that the ruler who is obviously a usurper, because it is more difficult to grapple with authority when it wrapped up in fine words and abstract arguments. The fact that we are able to vote for our rulers once every few years does not mean that we have to obey them for the rest of the time. If we do, it is for practical reasons not on moral grounds. Anarchists are against government, however it is constructed or defended.

State and Class

Anarchists have traditionally concentrated their opposition to authority on the state—that is, the institution which claims the monopoly of power within a certain area. This is because the state is the supreme example of authority in a society and also the source or confirmation of the use of authority throughout it. Moreover, anarchists have traditionally opposed all kinds of state—not just the obvious tyranny of a king, dictator or conqueror but also such variations as enlightened despotism, progressive monarchy, feudal or commercial oligarchy, parliamentary democracy, soviet communism and so on. Anarchists have even tended to say that all states are the same, and that there is nothing to choose between them.

This is an oversimplification. All states are certainly authoritarian, but some states are just as certainly more authoritarian than others, and every normal person would prefer to live under a less authoritarian rather than a more authoritarian one. To give a simple example, this statement of anarchism could not have been published under many states of the past, and it still could not be published under many states of both left and right, in both East and West, both North and South; I would rather live where it can be published and so would most of my readers.

Few anarchists still have such a simplistic attitude to an abstract thing called "the state", and anarchists concentrate on attacking the central government and the institutions which derive from it not just because they are part of the state, but because they are the extreme examples of the use of authority in society. We contrast the state with society, but we no longer see it as alien to society, as an artificial growth; instead we see it as part of society, as a natural growth. Authority is a normal form of behaviour, just as aggression is; but it is a form of behaviour which may and should be controlled and grown out of. This will not be done by trying to find ways of institutionalising it but only by finding ways of doing without it.

Anarchists object to the obviously repressive institutions of government—officials, laws, police, courts, prisons, armies and so on—and also to those which are apparently benevolent—subsidised bodies and local councils, nationalised industries and public corporations, banks and insurance companies, schools and universities, press and broadcasting, and all the rest. Anyone can see that the former depend not on consent but on compulsion and ultimately on force; anarchists insist that the latter have the same iron hand, even if it does wear a velvet glove.

Nevertheless, the institutions which derive directly or indirectly from the state cannot be understood if they are thought of as being merely bad. They can have a good side, in two ways. They have a useful negative function when they challenge the use of authority by other institutions, such as cruel parents, greedy landlords, brutal bosses, violent criminals; and they have a useful positive function when they promote desirable social activities, such as public works, disaster relief, communication and transport systems, art and culture, medical services, pension schemes, poor relief, education, broadcasting. Thus, we have the liberatory state and the welfare state, the state working for freedom and the state working for equality.

The first anarchist answer to this is that we primarily have the oppressive state—that the main function of the state is in fact to hold down the people, to limit freedom—and that all the benevolent functions of the state can be exercised and often have been exercised by voluntary associations. Here the modern states resembles the medieval church. In the Middle Ages the church was involved in all the essential social activities, and it was difficult to believe that the activities were possible without it. Only the church could baptise, marry and bury people, and they had to learn that it did not actually control birth, love and death. Every public act needed an official religious blessing—many still have one—and people had to learn that the act was just as effective without the blessing. The church interfered in and often controlled those aspects of communal life which are now dominated by the state. People have learnt to realise that the participation of the church is unnecessary and even harmful; what they now have to learn is that the domination of the state is equally pernicious and superfluous. We need the state just as long as we think we do, and everything it does can be done just as well or even better without the sanction of authority.

The second anarchist answer is that the essential function of the state is to maintain the existing inequality. Few anarchists agree with Marxists that the basic unit of society is the class, but most agree that the state is the political expression of the economic structure, that it is the representative of the people who own or control the wealth of the community and the oppressor of the people who do the work which creates the wealth. The state cannot redistribute wealth fairly, because it is the main agency of the unfair distribution. Anarchists agree with Marxists that the present system must be destroyed, but they do not agree that the future system can be established by a state in different hands; the state is a cause as well as a result of the class system, and a classless society which is established by a state will soon become a class society again. The state will not wither away—it must be deliberately abolished by people taking power away from the rulers and wealth away from the rich; these two actions are linked, and one without the other will always be futile. Anarchy in its truest sense means a society without either powerful or wealthy people.

Organisation and Bureaucracy

This does not mean that anarchists reject organisation, though here is one of the strongest prejudices about anarchism. People can accept that anarchy may not mean just chaos or confusion, and that anarchists want not disorder but order without government, but they are sure that anarchy means order which arises spontaneously and that anarchists do not want organisation. This is the reverse of the truth. Anarchists actually want much more organisation, though organisation without authority. The prejudice about anarchism derives from a prejudice about organisation; people cannot see that organisation does not depend on authority, that it actually works best without authority.

A moment's thought will show that when compulsion is replaced by consent there will have to be more discussion and planning, not less. Everyone who is involved in a decision will be able to take part in making it, and no one will be able to leave the work to paid officials or elected representatives. Without rules to observe or precedents to follow, every decision will have to be made afresh. Without rulers to obey or leaders to follow, we shall all have to make up our own minds. To keep all this going, the multiplicity and complexity of links between individuals will be increased, not reduced. Such organisation may be untidy and inefficient, but it will be much closer to the needs and feelings of the people concerned. If something cannot be done without the old kind of organisation, without authority and compulsion, it probably isn't worth doing and would be better left undone.

What anarchists do reject is the institutionalisation of organisation, the establishment of a special group of people whose function is to organise other people. Anarchist organisation would be fluid and open; as soon as organisation becomes hardened and closed, it falls into the hands of a bureaucracy, becomes the instrument of a particular class and reverts to the expression of authority instead of the coordination of society. Every group tends towards oligarchy, the rule of the few, and every organisation tends towards bureaucracy, the rule of the professionals; anarchists must always struggle against these tendencies, in the future as well as the present, and among themselves as well as among others.

Property

Nor do anarchists reject property, though we have a peculiar view of it. In one sense property is theft—that is, the exclusive appropriation of anything by anyone is a deprivation of everyone else. This does not mean that we are all communists; what it means is that any particular person's right to any particular thing depends not on whether that person made it or found it or bought it or was given it or is using it or wants it or has a legal right to it, but on whether that person needs it—and, more to the point, whether that person needs it more than someone else. This is a matter not of abstract justice or natural law but of human solidarity and obvious common sense. If I have a loaf of bread and you are hungry, it is yours not mine. If I have a coat and you are cold, it belongs to you. If I have a house and you have none, you have the right to use at least one of my rooms. But in another sense property is liberty—that is, the private enjoyment of goods and chattels in a sufficient quantity is an essential condition of the good life for the individual.

Anarchists are in favour of the private property which cannot be used by one person to exploit another— those personal possessions which we accumulate from childhood and which become part of our lives. What we are against is the public property which can be used only to exploit people—land and buildings, instruments of production and distribution, raw materials and manufactured articles, money and capital. The principle at issue is that people may be said to have a right to what they produce by their own labour but not to what they obtain from the labour of others; they have a right to what they need and use but not to what they do not need and cannot use. As soon as some people have more than enough, it either goes to waste or it stops other people having enough.

This means that rich people have no right to their property, for they are rich not because they work a lot, but because a lot of people work for them; and poor people have a right to rich people's property, for they are poor not because they work little, but because they work for others. Indeed, poor people almost always work longer hours at duller jobs in worse conditions than rich people. No one ever became rich or remained rich through their own labour, only by exploiting the labour of others. We may have a house and a piece of land, the tools of our trade and good health all our lives, and we may work as hard as we can as long as we can—we will produce enough for our families but little more; and even then we shall not be really self-sufficient, for we shall depend on others to provide some of our materials and to take of our produce in exchange.

Public property is not only a matter of ownership but also one of control. It is not necessary to possess property to exploit others. Rich people have always used other people to manage their property, and now that anonymous corporations and state enterprises are replacing individual property owners, managers are becoming the leading exploiters of other people's labour. In both developed and developing[2] countries, both capitalist and communist states, a tiny minority of the population still owns or otherwise controls the overwhelming proportion of public property.

Despite appearances, this is not an economic or legal problem. What matters is not the distribution of money or the system of land tenure or the organisation of taxation or the method of taxation or the law of inheritance, but the basic fact that some people will work for other people, just as some people will obey other people. If we refused to work for the rich and powerful, property would disappear—in the same way that, if we refused to obey rulers, authority would disappear. For anarchists, property is based on authority and not the other way round. The point is not how peasants put food into the landowners' mouths or how workers put money into the bosses' pockets but why they do so, and this is a political point.

Some people try to solve the problem of property by changing the law or the government, whether by reform or by revolution. Anarchists have no faith in such solutions, but they do not all agree on the right solution. Some anarchists want the division of everything among everyone, so that we all have an equal share in the world's wealth, and a *laissez-faire* commercial system with freed credit to prevent excessive accumulation. But most anarchists have no faith in this solution either and want the expropriation of all public property from those who have more than they need, so that we all have equal access to the world's wealth, and the control is in the hands of the whole community. But at least it is agreed that the present system of property must be destroyed together with the present system of authority.

---

2   Original text read "advanced and backwards". [editor]

God and the Church

Anarchists have traditionally been anticlerical and also atheist. The early anarchists were opposed to the church as much as to the state, and most of them have been opposed to religion itself. The slogan "Neither God nor master" has often been used to sum up the anarchist message. Many people still take the first step towards anarchism by abandoning their faith and becoming rationalists or humanists; the rejection of divine authority encourages the rejection of human authority. Nearly all anarchists today are probably atheists, or at least agnostics. But there have been religious anarchists, though they are usually outside the mainstream of the anarchist movement. Obvious examples are the heretical sects which anticipated some anarchist ideas before the nineteenth century and groups of religious pacifists in Europe and North America during the nineteenth and twentieth centuries, especially Tolstoy and his followers at the beginning of the twentieth century and the Catholic Worker movement in the United States since the 1930s.

The general anarchist hatred of religion has declined as the power of the church has declined, and most anarchists now think of it as a personal matter. They would oppose the discouragement of religion by force, but they would also oppose the revival of religion by force. They would let anyone believe and do what they want, so long as it affects only themselves; but they would not let the church have any more power.

War and Violence

Anarchists have always opposed war, but not all have opposed violence. They are anti-militarists but not necessarily pacifists. For anarchists, war is the supreme example of authority outside a society, and at the same time a powerful reinforcement of authority within society.

The organised violence and destruction of war are an enormously magnified version of the organised violence and destruction of the state, and war is the health of the state. The anarchist movement has a strong tradition of resistance to war and to preparations for war. A few anarchists have supported some wars, but they have always been recognised as renegades by their comrades, and this total opposition to national wars is one of the great unifying factors among anarchists.

But anarchists have distinguished between national wars between states and civil wars between classes. The revolutionary anarchist movement since the late nineteenth century has called for a violent insurrection to destroy the state, and anarchists have taken an active part in many armed risings and civil wars, especially those in Russia and Spain. Though they were involved in such fighting, however, they were under no illusions that it would itself bring about the revolution. Violence might be necessary for the work of destroying the old system, but it was useless and indeed dangerous for the work of building a new system. A people's army can defeat a ruling class and destroy a government, but it cannot help the people to create a free society, and it is no good winning a war if you cannot win the peace.

Many anarchists have in fact doubted whether violence plays any useful part at all. Like the state, it is not a neutral force whose effects depend on who uses it, and it will not do the right things just because it is in the right hands. Of course, the violence of the oppressed is not the same as the violence of the oppressor, but even when it is the best way out of an intolerable situation it is only a second best. It is one of the most unpleasant features of present society, and it remains unpleasant however good its purpose; moreover, it tends to destroy its purpose, even in situations where it seems appropriate—such as revolution. The experience of history suggests that revolutions are not guaranteed by violence; on the contrary, the more violence, the less revolution.

All this may seem absurd to people who are not anarchists. One of the oldest and most persistent prejudices about anarchism is that anarchists are above all men of violence. The stereotype of the anarchists with a bomb under his cloak is more than a century old, but it is still going strong. Many anarchists have indeed favoured violence, some have favoured the assassination of public figures, and a few have even favoured terrorism of the population, to help destroy the present system. There is a dark side to anarchism, and there is no point denying it. But it is only one side of anarchism, and a small one. Most anarchists have always opposed any violence except that which is really necessary—the inevitable violence which occurs when the people shake off their rulers and exploiters—though they may have been reluctant to condemn the few anarchists who have resorted to violence for sincere reasons.

The main perpetrators of violence have been those who maintain authority, not those who attack it. The great killers have not been the tragic bombers driven to desperation in southern Europe a century ago, but the military machines of every state in the world throughout history. No anarchist can rival the Blitz and the Bomb, no individual assassin can stand beside Hitler or Stalin. We would encourage workers to seize their factory or peasants to seize their land, and we might break fences or build barricades; but we have no soldiers, no aeroplanes, no police, no prisons, no camps, no firing squads, no gas chambers, no executioners. For anarchists, violence is the extreme example of the use of power by one person against another, the culmination of everything we are against.

In some cases anarchists have moved towards pacifism and pacifists have moved towards anarchism. this
has had beneficial results for both sides, anarchists learning from pacifism and pacifists learning from anarchists.
Some anarchists have been especially attracted by the
militant type of pacifism advocated by Tolstoy and Gandhi
and by the use of non-violence as a technique of direct
action, and many anarchists have taken part in anti-war
movements and have sometimes had a significant influence on them. But many anarchists—even those who are
closely involved—find pacifism too wide in its rejection
of all violence by all people in all circumstances, and too
narrow in its belief that the elimination of violence alone
will make a fundamental difference to society. Where
pacifists see authority as a weaker version of violence,
anarchists see violence a stronger version of authority.
Some anarchists are also repelled by the moralistic side of
pacifism, the asceticism and self-righteousness, and by
its tender-minded view of the world. To repeat, they are
anti-militarists but not necessarily pacifists.

The Individual and Society

The basic unit of society is the individual human being.
Nearly all individuals live in society, but society is
nothing more than a collection of individuals, and its
only purpose is to give them a full life. Anarchists do not
believe that people have natural rights, but this applies
to everyone; an individual has no right to do anything,
but no other individual has a right to stop that individual
doing anything. There is no general will, no social norm
to which we should conform. We are equal but not identical. Competition and cooperation, aggression and tender-
ness, intolerance and tolerance, violence and gentleness,
authority and rebellion—all these are natural forms of
social behaviour, but some help and others hinder the

full life of the individuals. Anarchists believe that the best way to guarantee it is to secure equal freedom for every member of society.

We therefore have no time for morality in the traditional sense, and we are not interested in what people do in their own lives. Let all individuals do exactly what they want, within the limits of their natural capacity, provided they let everyone else do exactly what *they* want. Such things as dress, appearance, speech, manners, acquaintance and so on, are matters of personal preference. So is sex. We are in favour of free love, but this does not mean that we advocate universal promiscuity; it means that all love is free, except prostitution and rape, and that people should be able to choose (or reject) forms of sexual behaviour and sexual partners for themselves. Extreme indulgence may suit one person, extreme chastity another—though most anarchists feel that the world would be a better place if there had been a lot less fussing and a lot more fucking. The same principle applies to such things as drugs. People can intoxicate themselves with alcohol or caffeine, cannabis or amphetamines, tobacco or opiates, and we have no right to prevent them, let alone punish them, though we may try to help them. Similarly, individuals can worship in their own way, so long as they let other individuals worship in their own way or not worship at all. It doesn't matter if people are offended, what does matter is if people are injured. There is no need to worry about differences in personal behaviour; the thing to worry about is the gross injustice of authoritarian society.

Anarchists have always opposed every form of national, social, racial or sexual oppression and have always supported every movement for national, social, racial or sexual emancipation. But they tend to differ from their allies in the movements by seeing all forms of oppression as being political in nature and in seeing all victims of oppression as individual human beings rather than as members of a nationality, class, race or sex.

The main enemy of the free individual is the overwhelming power of the state, but anarchists are also opposed to every other form of authority which limits freedom—in the family, in the school, at work, in the neighbourhood—and to every attempt to make the individual conform. However, before considering how society may be organised to give the greatest freedom to its members, it is necessary to describe the various forms anarchism has taken according to the various views of relationship between the individual and society.

■ How Anarchists Differ

Anarchists are notorious for disagreeing with each other, and in the absence of leaders and officials, hierarchies and orthodoxies, punishments and rewards, policies and programmes, it is natural that people whose fundamental principle is the rejection of authority should tend to perpetual dissent. Nevertheless, there are several well-established types of anarchism from which most anarchists have chosen one to express their particular view.

Philosophical Anarchism
The original type of anarchism was what is now called *philosophical* anarchism. This is the view that the idea of a society without government is attractive but not really desirable or desirable but not really possible, at least not yet. Such an attitude dominates all apparently anarchist writing before the 1840s, and it helped to prevent anarchic popular movements from becoming a more serious threat to governments. It is an attitude which is still found among many people who call themselves anarchists but remain outside any organised movement, and also among some people inside the anarchist movement. It is anarchism in the head but not in the heart, in theory but not in practice. Quite often it seems to be an almost unconscious attitude that anarchism, like the kingdom of God, is within you. It reveals itself sooner or later by some such phrase as, "Of course, I'm an anarchist, but. . ."

Active anarchists tend to despise philosophical anarchists, and this is understandable, though unfortunate. So long as anarchism is a minority movement, a general feeling in favour of anarchist ideas, however vague, creates a climate in which anarchist propaganda is listened to and the anarchist movement can grow. On the other hand, an acceptance of philosophical anarchism can inoculate people against an appreciation of real anarchism; but it is at least better than complete indifference. As well as philosophical anarchists, there are many people who are close to us but refuse to call themselves anarchists and some who refuse to call themselves anything at all. These all have their part to play, if only to provide a sympathetic audience and to work for freedom in their own lives.

Individualism, Egoism, Libertarianism

The first type of anarchism which was more than merely philosophical was *individualism*. This is the view that society is not an organism but a collection of autonomous individuals who have no obligation towards one another. This view existed long before there was any such thing as anarchism, and it has continued to exist quite separately from anarchism. But individualism always tends to assume that the individuals who make up society should be free and equal, and that they can become so only by their own efforts and not through the action of outside institutions; and any development of this attitude obviously brings mere individualism towards real anarchism.

The first person who elaborate a recognisable theory of anarchism—William Godwin, in his *Enquiry Concerning Political Justice* (1793)—was an individualist. In reaction against the opponents and also the supporters of the French Revolution, he postulated a society without government and with as little organisation as possible, in which the sovereign individuals should beware of any form of permanent association; despite many variations, this is a view of humanity which makes sense as far as it goes, but it doesn't go far enough to deal with the real problems of society, which surely need social rather than personal action. Alone, we may save ourselves, but others we cannot save.

A more extreme form of individualism is *egoism*, especially in the form expressed by Max Stirner in *Der Einzige und sein Eigentum* (1844)—usually translated as *The Ego and His Own*, though a better rendering would be *The Individual and His Property*. Like Marx or Freud, Stirner is difficult to interpret without offending all his followers; but it is perhaps acceptable to say that his egoism differs from individualism in general by rejecting such abstractions as morality, justice, obligation, reason and duty, in favour of an intuitive recognition of the existential uniqueness of each individual. It naturally opposes the state, but it also opposes society, and it tends towards nihilism (the view that nothing matters) and solipsism (the view that only oneself exists). It is clearly anarchist, but in a rather unproductive way, since any form of organisation beyond a temporary "union of egoists" is seen as the source of new oppression. This is an anarchism for poets and tramps, for people who want an absolute answer and no compromise. It is anarchy here and now, if not in the world, then in one's own life.

A more moderate tendency which derives from individualism is *libertarianism*. This is in its simplest sense the view that liberty is a good thing; in a stricter sense it is the view that freedom is the most important political goal. Thus, libertarianism is not so much a specific type of anarchism as a milder form of it, the first stage on the way to complete anarchism. Sometimes it is actually used as a synonym or euphemism for anarchism in general, when there is some reason to avoid the more emotive word; but it is more generally used to mean the acceptance of anarchist ideas in a particular field without the acknowledgement of anarchism as a whole. Individualists are libertarian by definition, but libertarian socialists or libertarian communists are those who bring to socialism or communism a recognition of the essential value of the individual.

Mutualism and Federalism

The type of anarchism which appears when individualists begin to put their ideas into practice is *mutualism*. This is the view that, instead of relying on the state, society should be organised by individuals entering into voluntary agreements with each other on a basis of equality and reciprocity. Mutualism is a feature of any association which is more than instinctive and less than official, and it is not necessarily anarchist, but it was historically important in the development of anarchism, and nearly all anarchist proposals for the reorganisation of society have been essentially mutualist.

The first person who deliberately called himself an anarchist—Pierre-Joseph Proudhon, in *What is Property?* (1840)—was a mutualist. In reaction against the utopian and revolutionary socialists of the early nineteenth century, he postulated a society made up of cooperative groups of free individuals exchanging the necessities of life on the basis of labour value and exchanging free credit through a people's bank. This is an anarchism for craftsmen and artisans, for smallholders and shopkeepers, professionals and specialists, for people who like to work on equal terms but stand on their own two feet. Despite his disclaimers, Proudhon had many followers, especially among the skilled working class and the lower middle class, and his influence was considerable in France during the second half of the nineteenth century; mutualism also had a particular appeal in North America, and to a lesser extent in Britain. It later tended to be taken up by the sort of people who favour currency reform or self-sufficient communities—measures of a kind which promise quick results but do not affect the basic structure of society. This is a view of humanity which makes sense as far as it goes, but it doesn't go far enough to deal with such things as industry and capital, the class system which dominates them or—above all—the state.

Mutualism is of course the principle of the cooperative movement, but cooperative societies are run on democratic rather than anarchist lines. A society organised according to the principle of anarchist mutualism would be one in which communal activities were in effect in the hands of cooperative societies without permanent managers or elected officials. Economic mutualism may thus be seen as cooperativism minus bureaucracy, or as capitalism minus profit.

Mutualism expressed geographically rather than economically becomes *feudalism*. This is the view that society in a wider sense than the local community should be coordinated by a network of councils which are drawn from the various areas and which are themselves coordinated by councils covering wider areas. The essential feature of anarchist federalism is that the members of such councils would be delegates without any executive authority, subject to instant recall, and that the councils would have no central authority, only a simple secretariat. Proudhon, who first elaborated mutualism, also first elaborated federalism—in *The Federal Principle* (1863)—and his followers were called federalists as well as mutualists, especially those who were active in the labour movement; thus the figures in the early history of the First International and in the Paris Commune who anticipated the ideas of the modern anarchist movement mostly described themselves as federalists.

Federalism is not so much a type of anarchism as an inevitable part of anarchism. Virtually all anarchists are federalists but virtually none would define themselves only as federalists. Federalism is after all a common principle which is by no means confined to the anarchist movement. There is nothing utopian about it. The international systems for coordinating railways, shipping, air traffic, postal services, telegraphs and telephones, scientific research, famine relief, disaster operations and many other worldwide activities are essentially federalist in structure. Anarchists simply add that such systems would work just as well within as they do between countries. After all, this is already true of the overwhelming proportion of voluntary societies, associations and organisations of all kinds which handle those social activities which are not financially profitable or politically sensitive.

Collectivism, Communism, Syndicalism

The type of anarchism which goes further than individualism or mutualism and involves a direct threat to the class system and the state is what used to be called *collectivism*. This is the view that society can be reconstructed only when the working class seizes control of the economy by a social revolution, destroys the state apparatus and reorganises production on the basis of common ownership and control by associations of working people. The instruments of labour would be held in common, but the products of labour would be distributed on the principle of the slogan used by some French socialists during the 1840s, "From each according to his ability, to each according to his work".

The first modern anarchists—the Bakuninists in the First International—were collectivists. In reaction against the reformist mutualists and federalists and also against the authoritarian Blanquists and Marxists, they

postulated a simple form of revolutionary anarchism—
the anarchism of the class struggle and the proletariat,
of the mass insurrection of the poor against the rich and
the immediate transition to a free and classless society
without any intermediate period of dictatorship. This is
an anarchism for class-conscious workers and peasants,
for militants and activists in the labour movement, for
socialists who want liberty as well as equality.

This anarchist or revolutionary collectivism must
not be confused with the better-known authoritarian
and reformist collectivism of the Social Democrats and
Fabians—the collectivism which is based on common
ownership of the economy but also on state control of production and distribution. Partly because of the danger of
this confusion, and partly because it is here that anarchists and socialists come closest to each other, a better
description of this type of anarchism is libertarian socialism—which includes not only anarchists who are socialists but also socialists who lean towards anarchism but
are not quite anarchists.

The type of anarchism which appears when collectivism is worked out in more detail is *communism*. This is the
view that it is not enough for the instruments of labour
to be held in common, but that the products of labour
should also be held in common and distributed on the
principle of the slogan used by other French socialists
during the 1840s, "From each according to his ability, to
each according to his needs". The communist argument
is that, while people are entitled to the full value of their
labour, it is impossible to calculate the value of any individual's labour, for the work of each is involved in the
work of all, and different kinds of work have different
kinds of value. It is therefore better for the entire economy
to be in the hands of society as a whole and for the wage
and price system to be abolished.

Almost all the leading figures of the anarchist movement at the end of the nineteenth century and the beginning of the twentieth century—such as Kropotkin, Malatesta, Reclus, Grave, Faure, Goldman, Berkman, Rocker and so on—were communists. Going on from collectivism and reacting against Marxism, they postulated a more sophisticated form of revolutionary anarchism—the anarchism containing the most carefully considered criticism of present society and proposals for future society. This is an anarchism for those who accept the class struggle but have a wider view of the world. If collectivism is revolutionary anarchism concentrating on the problem of work and based on the workers' collective, then communism is revolutionary anarchism concentrating on the problem of life and based on the people's commune.

Since the 1870s, the principle of communism has been accepted by most anarchist organisations favouring revolution. The main exception was the movement in Spain, which retained the principle of collectivism because of strong Bakuninists influence; but, in fact, its aims were scarcely different from those of other movements, and in practice the "*comunismo libertario*" established during the Spanish Revolution in 1936 was the most impressive example of anarchist communism in history.

This anarchist or libertarian communism must of course not be confused with the much better-known communism of the Marxists—the communism which is based on the common ownership of the economy and state control of production, distribution and consumption, and also of party dictatorship. The historical origin of the modern anarchist movement in the dispute with the Marxists in the First and Second Internationals is reflected in the ideological obsession of anarchists with authoritarian communism, and this has been reinforced since the Russian and Spanish revolutions. As a result, many anarchists seem to have called themselves communists not so much from definite conviction but more from a wish to challenge the Marxists on their own ground and outdo them in the eyes of public opinion. One may suspect that anarchists are seldom really communist, partly because they are always too individualist and partly because they would not wish to lay down elaborate plans for a future which must be free to make its own arrangements.

The type of anarchism which appears when collectivism or communism concentrates exclusively on the problem of work in *syndicalism*. This is the view that society should be based on the trade unions, as the expression of the working class, reorganised so as to cover both occupations and areas, and reformed so as to be in the hands of the rank and file, so that the whole economy is managed according to the principle of workers' control.

Most anarchist collectivists and many communists during the nineteenth century were syndicalists by implication, and this was particularly true of the anarchists in the First International. But anarcho-syndicalism was not developed explicitly until the rise of the French syndicalist movement at the end of the century. (The English word "syndicalism" comes from the French word *syndicalisme*, which simply means trade unionism.) When the French trade union movement divided into revolutionary and reformist sections in the 1890s, the revolutionary syndicalists became dominant, and many anarchists joined them. Some of these, such as Fernand Pelloutier and Emile Pouget, became influential, and the French syndicalist movement, though never fully anarchist, was a powerful force for anarchism until the First World War and the Russian Revolution. Anarcho-syndicalist organisations were also strong in the labour movements of Italy and Russia just after the First World War, in Latin

America and above all in Spain until the end of the Civil War in 1939.

This is an anarchism for the most class-conscious and militant elements in a strong labour movement. But syndicalism is not necessarily anarchist or even revolutionary; in practice anarcho-syndicalists have tended to become authoritarian or reformist, or both, and it has proved difficult to maintain a balance between libertarian principles and the pressures of the day-to-day struggle for better pay and conditions. This is not so much an argument against anarcho-syndicalism as a constant danger for anarcho-syndicalists. The real argument against anarcho-syndicalism and against syndicalism in general is that it overemphasises the importance of work and the function of the working class. The class system is a central political problem, but the class struggle is not the only political activity for anarchists. Syndicalism is acceptable when it is seen as one aspect of anarchism but not when it obscures all other aspects. This is a view of humanity which makes sense as far as it goes, but it doesn't go far enough to deal with life outside work.

Not So Different

It must be said that the differences between various types of anarchism have become less important in recent years. Except for dogmatists at each extreme, most anarchists tend to see the old distinctions as more apparent than real—as artificial differences of emphasis, even of vocabulary, rather than as serious differences of principle. It might in fact be better to think of them as not so much types as aspects of anarchism which depend on the direction of our interests.

Thus in our private lives we are individualists, doing our own things and choosing our companions and friends for personal reasons; in our social lives we are mutualists, making free agreements with each other and giving what we have and getting what we need by equal exchanges with each other; in our working lives we would mostly be collectivists, joining our colleague in producing for the common good—and in the management of work we would mostly be syndicalists, joining our colleagues in deciding how the job should be done; in our political lives we would mostly be communists, joining our neighbours in deciding how the community should be run. This is of course a simplification, but it expresses a general truth about the way anarchists think nowadays.

■ What Anarchists Want

It is difficult to say what anarchists want, not just because they differ so much, but because they hesitate to make detailed proposals about a future which they are neither able nor willing to control. After all, anarchists want a society without government, and such a society would obviously vary widely from time to time and from place to place. The whole point of the society anarchists want is that it would be what its members themselves want. Nevertheless, it is possible to say what most anarchists would like to see in a free society, though it must always be remembered that there is no official line and also no way of reconciling the extremes of individualism and communism.

The Free Individual

Most anarchists begin with a libertarian attitude towards private life and want a much wider choice for personal behaviour and for social relationships between individuals. But if the individual is the atom of society, the family is the molecule, and family life would continue even if all the coercion enforcing it were removed. Nevertheless, though the family may be natural, it is no longer necessary; efficient contraception and intelligent division of labour have released humanity from the narrow choice between celibacy and monogamy. There is no need for a couple to have children, and children may be brought up by more or less than two parents. People may live alone and still have sexual partners and children or live in communes with no permanent partnerships or official parenthood at all.

No doubt most people will go on practising some form of marriage and most children will be brought up in a family environment, whatever happens to society, but there could be a great variety of personal arrangements within a single community. The fundamental requirement is that women should be freed from the oppression of men, and that children should be freed from the oppression of parents. The exercise of authority is no better in the microcosm of the family than in the macrocosm of society.

Personal relationships outside the family would be regulated not by arbitrary laws or economic competition but by the natural solidarity of the human species. Almost all of us know how to treat other people—as we would like them to treat us—and self-respect and public opinion are far better guides to action that fear or guilt. Some opponents of anarchism have suggested that the moral oppression of society would be worse than the physical oppression of the state, but a greater danger is surely the unregulated authority of the vigilante group, the lynch mob, the robber band or the criminal gang—the rudimentary forms of the state which come to the surface when the regulated authority of the real state is for some reason absent.

But anarchists disagree little about private life, and there is not much of a problem here. After all, a great many people have already made their own new arrangements, without waiting for a revolution or anything else. All that is needed for the liberation of the individual is the emancipation from old prejudices and the achievement of a certain standard of living. The real problem is the liberation of society.

The Free Society

The first priority of a free society would be the abolition of authority and the expropriation of property. In place of government by permanent representatives who are subject to occasional election and by career bureaucrats who are virtually unmoveable, anarchists want coordination by temporary delegates who are subject to instant recall and by professional experts who are genuinely accountable. In such a system, all those social activities which involve organisation would probably be managed by free associations. These might be called councils or cooperatives or collectives or communes or committees or unions or syndicates or soviets or anything else—their title would be irrelevant; the important thing would be their function.

There would be work associations from the workshop or smallholding up the largest industrial or agricultural complex to handle the production and transport of goods, decide conditions of work and run the economy. There would be area associations from the neighbourhood or village up to the largest residential unit to handle the life of the community—housing, streets, refuse, amenities. There would be associations to handle the social aspects of such activities as communications, culture, recreation, research, health and education.

One result of coordination by free association rather than administration by established hierarchies would be extreme decentralisation on federalist lines. This may seem an argument against anarchism, but we would say that it is an argument for it. One of the oddest things about modern political thought is that wars are often blamed on the existence of many small nations when the worst wars in history have been caused by a few large ones. Governments are always trying to create larger and larger administrative units when observation suggests

that the best ones are small. The breakdown of big political systems would be one of the greatest benefits of anarchism, and countries could become cultural entities once
more, while nations would disappear.

The association concerned with any kind of wealth
or property would have the crucial responsibility of either
making sure that it was fairly divided among the people
involved or else of holding it in common and making
sure that the use of it was fairly shared among the people
involved. Anarchists differ about which system is best,
and no doubt the members of a free society would also
differ; it would be up to the people in each association
to adopt whichever method they preferred. There might
be equal pay for all or pay according to need or no pay at
all. Some associations might use money for all exchange,
some just for large or complex transactions and some
might not use it at all. Goods might be bought or hired or
rationed or free. If this sort of speculation seems absurdly
unrealistic or utopian, it may be worth remembering just
how much we already hold in common and how many
things may be used without payment.

In Britain, the community owns some heavy industries, air and rail transport, ferries and buses, broadcasting systems, water, gas and electricity, though we pay
to use them; but roads, bridges, rivers, beaches, parks,
libraries, playgrounds, lavatories, schools, universities,
hospitals and emergency services are not only owned by
the community but may be used without payment. The
distinction between what is owned privately and what is
owned communally and between what may be used for
payment and what may be used freely is quite arbitrary.
It may seem obvious that we should be able to use roads
and beaches without payment, but this was not always
the case, and the free use of hospitals and universities
has come only during this century. In the same way, it

may seem obvious that we should pay for transport and fuel, but this may not always be the case, and there is no reason why they should not be free.

One result of the equal division or free distribution of wealth rather than the accumulation of property would be the end of the class system based on ownership. But anarchists also want to end the class system based on control. This would mean constant vigilance to prevent the growth of bureaucracy in every association, and above all it would mean the reorganisation of work without a managerial class.

Work

The first need of every human being is for food, shelter and clothing, which make life liveable; the second is for the further comforts, which make life worth living. The prime economic activity of any human group is the production and distribution of the things which satisfy these needs; and the most important aspect of a society—after the personal relations on which it is based—is the organisation of the necessary work. Anarchists have two characteristic ideas about work: the first is that most work may be unpleasant but could be organised to be more bearable and even pleasurable; and the second is that all work should be organised by the people who actually do it.

Anarchists agree with Marxists that work in present society alienates workers. It is not their life but what they do to be able to live; their life is what they do outside work, and when they do something they enjoy they do not call it work. This is true of most work for most people in all places, and it is bound to be true of a lot of work for a lot of people at all times. The tiring and repetitive labour which has to be done to make plants grow and animals thrive, to run production lines and transport systems, to get to people what they want and take from them what they do not want, could not be abolished without a drastic decline in the material standard of living; and automation, which can make it less tiring, makes it even more repetitive. But anarchists insist that the solution is not to condition people into believing that the situation is inevitable but to reorganise essential labour so that, in the first place, it is normal for everyone who is capable of it to take a share in doing it and for no one to spend more than a few hours a day on it; and so that, in the second place, it is possible for everyone to alternate between different kinds of boring labour, which would become less boring through greater variety. It is a matter not just of fair shares for all but also of fair work for all.

Anarchists also agree with syndicalists that work should be run by the workers. This does not mean that the working class—or the trade unions or a working-class party (that is, a party claiming to represent the working class)—runs the economy and has ultimate control of work. Nor does it mean the same thing on a smaller scale, that the staff of a factory can elect managers or see the account. It means quite simply that the people doing a particular job are in direct and total control of what they do, without any bosses or managers or inspectors at all. Some people may be good coordinators, and they can concentrate on coordination, but there is no need for them to have power over the people who do the actual work. Some people may be lazy or inefficient, but they are already. The point is to have the greatest possible control over one's own work, as well as one's own life.

This principle applies to all kinds of work—in fields as well as factories, in large concerns as well as small, in unskilled as well as skilled occupations, and in dirty jobs as well as liberal professions—and it is not just a useful gesture to make workers happy but a fundamental principle of any kind of free economy. An obvious objection is that complete workers' control would lead to wasteful competition between different workplaces and to pro- duction of unwanted things; an obvious answer is that complete lack of workers' control leads to exactly the same things. What is needed is intelligent planning, and despite what most people seem to thing, this depends not on more control from above but on more information from below, on horizontal rather than vertical communication.

Most economists have been concerned with produc- tion rather than consumption—with the manufacture of things rather than their use. Right-wingers and left- wingers both want workers to produce more, whether to make the rich richer or to make the state stronger, and the result is "overproduction" alongside poverty, growing productivity together with growing unemployment, higher blocks of offices at the same time as increasing homelessness, greater yields of crops per acre when more acres are left uncultivated. Anarchists are concerned with consumption rather than production—with the use of things to satisfy the needs of the whole people instead of to increase the profits and power of the rich and strong.

Necessities and Luxuries

A society with any pretension to decency cannot allow the exploitation of basic needs. It may be acceptable for luxuries to be bought and sold, since we have a choice whether we use them or not, but necessities are not mere commodities, since we have no choice about using them. If anything should be taken off the commercial market and out of the hands of exclusive groups, it is surely the land we live on, the food which grows on it, the homes which are built on it and those essential things which make up the material basis of human life—clothes, tools, amenities, fuel and so on. It is also surely obvious that when there is plenty of any necessity everyone should be able to take what is needed; but that when there is a scarcity, there should be a freely agreed system of rationing so that everyone gets a fair share. It is clear that there is something wrong with any system in which waste and want exist side by side, in which some people have more than they need while other people have less.

Above all it is clear that the first task of a healthy society is to eliminate the scarcity of necessities—such as the lack of food in undeveloped countries and the lack of housing in advanced countries—by the proper use of technical knowledge and of social resources. If the available skill and labour in Britain were used properly, for instance, there is no reason why enough food could not be grown and enough homes could not be built to feed and house the whole population. It does not happen now because present society has other priorities, not because it cannot happen. At one time it was assumed that it was impossible for everyone to be clothed properly, and poor people always wore rags; now there are plenty of clothes, and there could be plenty of everything else too.

Luxuries, by a strange paradox, are also necessities, though not basic necessities. The second task of a healthy society is to make luxuries freely available as well, though this may be a place where money would still have a useful function—provided it were not distributed according to the ludicrous lack of system in capitalist countries or the even more ludicrous system in communist ones. The essential point is that everyone should have free and equal access to luxury.

But man does not live by bread alone, or even by cake. Anarchists would not like to see recreational, intellectual, cultural and other such activities in the hands of society—even the most libertarian society. But there are other activities which cannot be left to individuals in free associations but must be handled by society as a whole.

These are what may be called welfare activities—mutual aid beyond the reach of family and friends and outside the place of residence or work. Let us consider three of these.

The Welfare Society

Education is very important in human society, because we take so long to grow and take so long learning facts and skills necessary for social life, and anarchists have always been much concerned about the problems of education. Many anarchist leaders have made valuable contributions to educational theory and practice, and many educational reformers have had libertarian tendencies—from Rousseau and Pestalozzi to Montessori and Neill. Ideas about education which were once thought of as utopian are now a normal part of the curriculum both inside and outside the state educational systems in Britain, and education is perhaps the most stimulating area of society for practical anarchists.

When people say that anarchy sounds nice but cannot work, we can point to a good school or college, or a good adventure playground or youth club. But even the best educational system is still under the control of people in authority—teachers, administrators, governors, officials, inspectors and so on. The adults concerned in any educational process are bound to dominate it to some extent, but there is no need for them—let alone people not directly concerned in it at all—to control it.

Anarchists want the current educational reforms to go much further. Not only should strict discipline and corporal punishment be abolished—so should all imposed discipline and all penal methods. Not only should educational institutions be freed from the power of outside authorities, but students should be freed from the power of teachers or administrators. In a healthy educational relationship the fact that one person knows more than another is no reason for the teacher to have authority over the learner. The status of teachers in present society is based on age, strength, experience and law; the only status teachers should have would be based on their knowledge of a subject and their ability to teach it, and ultimately on their capacity to inspire admiration and respect. What is needed is not so much student power—though that is a useful corrective to teachers' power and bureaucrats' power—as workers' control by all the people involved in an educational institution. The essential point is to break the link between teaching and governing and to make education free.

This break is actually nearer in health than in education. Doctors are no longer magicians, and nurses are no longer saints, and in many countries—including Britain—the right of free medical treatment is accepted. What is needed is the extension of the principle of freedom from the economic to the political side of the health system. People should be able to go to hospital without any payment, and people should also be able to work in hospitals without any hierarchy. Once again, what is needed is workers' control by all the people involved in a medical institution. And just as education is for students, so health is for patients.

The treatment of delinquency has also progressed a long way, but it is still far from satisfactory. Anarchists have two characteristic ideas about delinquency: the first is that most so-called criminals are much the same as other people, just poorer, weaker, sillier or unluckier; the second is that people who persistently hurt other people should not be hurt in turn but should be looked after. The biggest criminals are not burglars but bosses, not gangsters but rulers, not murderers but mass murderers. A few minor injustices are exposed and punished by the state, while the many major injustices of present society are disguised and actually perpetuated by the state. In general punishment does more damage to society than crime does; it is more extensive, better organised and much more effective. Nevertheless, even the most libertarian society would have to protect itself against some people, and this would inevitably involve some compulsion. But proper treatment of delinquency would be part of the education and health system and would not become an institutionalised system of punishment. The last resort would not be imprisonment or death but boycott or expulsion.

Pluralism

This might work the other way. Some individuals or groups might refuse to join or insist on leaving the best possible society; there would be nothing to stop them. In theory it is possible for us to support ourselves by our own efforts, though in practice we would depend on the community to provide some materials and to take some products in exchange, so it is difficult to be literally self-sufficient. A collectivist or communist society should tolerate and even encourage such pockets of individualism. What would be unacceptable would be independent individuals trying to exploit other people's labour by employing them at unfair wages or exchanging goods at unfair prices. This should not happen, because people would not normally work or buy for someone else's benefit rather than their own; and while no law would prevent appropriation, no law would prevent expropriation either—you could take something from someone else, but they could take it back again. Authority and property could hardly be restored by isolated individuals.

A greater danger would come from independent groups. A separate community could easily exist within society, and this might cause severe strains; if such a community reverted to authority and property, which might make it stronger and richer, there would be a temptation for people to join the secession, especially if society at large were going through a bad time.

But a free society would have to be pluralist and put up with not only minor differences of opinion about how freedom and equality should be put into practice but also with major deviations from the theory of freedom and equality altogether. The only condition would be that no people are forced to join such tendencies against their will, and here some kind of authoritarian pressure would have to be available to protect even the most libertarian society. But anarchists want to replace mass society by a mass of societies, all living together as freely as the individuals within them. The greatest danger to the free societies that have been established has been not internal regression but external aggression, and the real problem is not so much how to keep a free society going as how to get it going in the first place.

Revolution or Reform

Anarchists have traditionally advocated a violent revolution to establish a free society, but some have rejected violence or revolution or both—violence is so often followed by counter-violence and revolution by counter-revolution. On the other hand, few anarchists have advocated mere reform, realising that while the system of authority and property exists superficial changes will never threaten the basic structures of society. The difficulty is that what anarchists want is revolutionary, but a revolution will not necessarily—or even probably—lead to what anarchists want. This is why anarchists have tended to resort to desperate actions or to relapse into hopeless inactivity.

In practice most disputes between reformist and revolutionary anarchists are meaningless, for only the wildest revolutionary refuses to welcome reforms and the mildest reformists refuses to welcome revolutions, and all revolutionaries know that their work will generally lead to no more than reform, and all reformists know that their work is generally leading to some kind of revolution. What most anarchists want is a constant pressure of all kinds, bringing about the conversion of individuals, the formation of groups, the reform of institutions, the rising of the people and the destruction of authority and property. If this happened without trouble, we would be delighted, but it never has, and it probably never will. In the end, it is necessary to go out and confront the forces of the state in the neighbourhood, at work and in the streets—and if the state is defeated it is even more necessary to go on working to prevent the establishment of a new state and to begin the construction of a free society instead. There is a place for everyone in this process, and all anarchists find something to do in the struggle for what they want.

■ What Anarchists Do

Anarchists begin by thinking and talking. Few people begin as anarchists, and becoming an anarchist tends to be a confusing experience which involves a considerable emotional and intellectual upheaval. Being a conscious anarchist is a continuously difficult situation (rather like being, say, an atheist in medieval Europe); it is difficult to break through the thought barrier and persuade people that the necessity for government (like the existence of God) is not self-evident but may be discussed and even rejected. An anarchist has to work out a whole new view of the world and a new way of dealing with it; this is usually done in conversation with people who are anarchists or are near to anarchism, especially within some left-wing group or activity.

Afterwards, even the most single-minded anarchist has contact with non-anarchists, and such contract is inevitably an opportunity for spreading anarchist ideas. Among family and friends, at home and at work, any anarchists who are not entirely philosophical in their convictions are bound to be influenced by them. It is not universal but it is usual for anarchists to be less worried than other people about such things as faithfulness in their spouses, obedience in their children, conformity in their neighbours or punctuality in their colleagues. Anarchist employees and citizens are less likely to do what they are told, and anarchist teachers and parents are less likely to make others do what they are told. Anarchism which does not show in personal life is pretty unreliable.

Some anarchists are content with making up their own minds and confining their opinions to their own lives, but most want to go further and influence other people. In conversation about social or political matters they will put the libertarian point of view, and in struggles over public issues they will support the libertarian solution. But to make a real impact it is necessary to work with other anarchists or in some kind of political group on a more permanent basis than chance encounter. This is the beginning of organisation, leading to propaganda, and finally to action.

Organisation and Propaganda

The initial form of anarchist organisation is a discussion group. If this proves viable, it will develop in two ways—it will establish links with other groups, and it will begin wider activity. Links with other groups may eventually lead to some sort of federation which can coordinate activity and undertake more ambitious enterprises. Anarchist activity normally begins with some form of propaganda to get across the basic idea of anarchism itself. There are two main ways of doing this—*propaganda by word* and *propaganda by deed*.

The word may be written or spoken. Nowadays the spoken word is heard less than it used to be, but public meetings—whether indoors or in the open—are still a valuable method of reaching people directly. The final stage in becoming an anarchist is normally precipitated by some kind of personal contact, and a meeting is a good opportunity for this. As well as holding specifically anarchist meetings, it is also worth attending other meetings to put an anarchist point of view, whether by taking part in the proceedings or by interrupting them.

The most sophisticated vehicle for the spoken word nowadays is of course radio and television, and anarchists have occasionally managed to get a hearing on some programmes. But broadcasting is in fact a rather unsatisfactory medium for propaganda, because it is unsuitable for conveying unfamiliar ideas, and anarchism is still an unfamiliar idea for most listeners and viewers: it is also unsuitable for conveying explicit political ideas, and anarchism is probably broadcast most effectively in the form of implicit morals to stories. The same is true of such media as the cinema and the theatre, which can be used for extremely effective propaganda in skilful hands. In general, however, anarchists have not been able to make as much of these channels of communication as one might hope.

Anyway, however effective propaganda by speech may be, the written word is necessary to fill out the message, and this has been and still is by far the most common form of propaganda. The idea of society without government may have existed underground for centuries and occasionally come to the surface in radical popular movements, but it was first brought out into the open for thousands of people by the books of the such writers as Paine, Godwin, Proudhon, Stirner and so on. And when the idea took root and was expressed by organised groups, there began that flood of periodicals and pamphlets which is still the main method of communication in the anarchist movement. Some of these publications have been very good; most have been rather bad; but they have all been essential in making sure that the movement has not turned in on itself but has maintained a constant dialogue with the external world. Again, as well as producing specifically anarchist works, it is also worth contributing to non-anarchist periodicals and writing non-anarchist books to put an anarchist point of view to non-anarchist readers.

But the spoken and written word, though necessary, are never sufficient. We can talk and write in general term as much we like, but by itself that will get us nowhere. It is also necessary to move beyond mere propaganda in two ways—to discuss particular issues at such a time and in such a manner as to have an immediate effect or to win publicity by something more dramatic than mere words. The first way is agitation, the second is propaganda by deed.

Agitation is the point at which a political theory encounters political reality. Anarchist agitation becomes suitable when people are made especially receptive to anarchist ideas because of some kind of stress in the state system—during national or civil wars, industrial or agrarian struggles, campaigns against oppression or public scandals—and it consists essentially of propaganda brought down to earth and made practicable. In a situation of growing consciousness, people are not so much interested in general speculation as in specific proposals. This is the opportunity to show in detail what is wrong with the present system and how it could be put right. Anarchist agitation has sometimes been effective, especially in France, Spain, parts of Latin America and the United States before the First World War, in Russia, Italy and China after it, and in Spain during the 1930s; it has occasionally been effective in Britain, in the 1880s, in the early 1940s and again from the 1960s.

The idea of propaganda by deed is often misunderstood, by anarchists as well as their enemies. When the phrase was first used (during the 1870s) it meant demonstrations, riots and risings which were thought of as symbolic actions designed to win useful publicity rather than immediate success. The point was that the propaganda would consist not just of talk about what could be done but of news about what had been done. It did not originally and does not necessarily mean violence, let alone assassination; but after the wave of outrages by individual anarchists during the 1890s, propaganda by deed became popularly identified with personal acts of violence, and this image has not yet faded.

For most anarchists nowadays, however, propaganda by deed is more likely to be non-violent, or at least un-violent, and to be against bombs rather than with them. It has in fact reverted to its original meaning, though it now tends to take rather different forms—sit-downs and sit-ins, organised heckling and unorthodox demonstrations. Propaganda by deed need not be illegal, though it often is. Civil disobedience is a special type of propaganda by deed which involves the open and deliberate breaking of a law to gain publicity. Many anarchists dislike it, because it also involves the open and deliberate invitation of punishment, which offends anarchist feelings about any kind of voluntary contact with the authorities; but there have been times when some anarchists have found it a useful form of propaganda.

Agitation, especially when it is successful, and propaganda by deed, especially when it is illegal, both go further than mere propaganda. Agitation incites action, and propaganda by deed involves action; it is here that anarchists move into the field of action and that anarchism begins to become serious.

Action

The change from theorising about anarchism to putting it into practice means a change in organisation. The typical discussion or propaganda group, which is open to easy participation by outsiders and easy observation by the authorities, and which is based on all members doing what they want to do and not doing what they don't want to do, will become more exclusive and more formal. This is a moment of great danger, since an attitude which is too rigid leads to authoritarianism and sectarianism, while one which is too lax leads to confusion and irresponsibility. It is a moment of even greater danger, since when anarchism becomes a serious matter, anarchists become a serious threat to the authorities and real persecution begins.

The most common form of anarchist action is for agitation over an issue to become participation in a campaign. This may be reformist, for something which would not change the whole system, or revolutionary, for a change in the system itself; it may be legal or illegal or both, violent or non-violent or just un-violent. It may have a chance of success, or it may be hopeless from the start. The anarchists may be influential or even dominant in the campaign, or they may be only one of many groups taking part. It does not take long to think of a wide variety of possible fields of action, and for a century anarchists have tried them all. The form of action with which anarchists have been happiest and which is most typical of anarchism is *direct action*.

The idea of direct action is also often misunderstood, by anarchists as well as their enemies, again. When the phrase was first used (during the 1890s) it meant no more than the opposite of "political"—that is, parliamentary—action; and in the context of the labour movement it meant "industrial" action, especially strikes, boycotts and sabotage, which were thought of as preparations for and rehearsals of revolution. The point was that the action is applied not indirectly through representatives but directly by the people most closely involved in a situation and directly on the situation, and it is intended to win some measure of success rather than mere publicity.

This would seem clear enough, but direct action has in fact been confused with propaganda by deed, and especially with civil disobedience. The technique of direct action was actually developed in the French syndicalist movement in reaction against the more extreme techniques of propaganda by deed; instead of getting sidetracked into dramatic but ineffective gestures, the trade unionists got on with the dull but effective work—that at least was the theory. But as the syndicalist movement grew and came into conflict with the system in France, Spain, Italy, the United States and Russia, and even Britain, the high points of direct action began to take on the same function as acts of propaganda by deed. Then, when Gandhi began to describe as direct action what was really a non-violent form of civil disobedience, all three phrases were confused and came to mean much the same—more or less any form of political activity which is against the law or otherwise outside the accepted rules of constitutional etiquette.

For most anarchists, however, direct action still has its original meaning, though as well as its traditional forms it also takes new ones—invading military bases or taking over universities, squatting in houses or occupying factories. What makes it particularly attractive to anarchists is that it is consistent with libertarian principles and also with itself. Most forms of political action by opposition groups are mainly designed to win power; some groups use the techniques of direct action, but as soon as they win power they not only stop using such techniques but prevent any other groups using them either. Anarchists are in favour of direct action at all times, they see it as normal action, as action which reinforces itself and grows as it is used, as action which can be used to create and also to sustain a free society.

But there are some anarchists who have no faith in the possibility of creating a free society, and their action varies accordingly. One of the strongest pessimistic tendencies in anarchism is *nihilism*. Nihilism was the word which Turgenev coined (in his novel *Father and Sons*) to describe the sceptical and scornful attitude of the young populists in Russia a century ago, but it came to mean the view which denies the value not only of the state or of prevailing morality but of society and of humanity itself; for the strict nihilist nothing is sacred, not even himself—so nihilism is one step beyond the most thorough egoism.

An extreme form of action inspired by nihilism is *terrorism* for its own sake rather than for revenge or propaganda. Anarchists have no monopoly of terror, but it has sometimes been fashionable in some sections of the movement. After the frustrating experience of preaching a minority theory in hostile or often indifferent society, it is tempting to attack society physically. It may not do much about the hostility, but it will certainly end the indifference; let them hate me, so long as they fear me, is the terrorist's line of thought. But if reasoned assassination has been unproductive, random terror has been counterproductive, and it is not too much to say that nothing has done more damage to anarchism than the streak of psychopathic violence which always ran and still runs through it.

A milder form of action inspired by nihilism is *bohemianism*, which is a constant phenomenon, though the name seems to change for each manifestation. This too has been fashionable in some sections of the anarchist movement, and, of course, far outside as well. Instead of attacking society, bohemians drop out of it—though, while living without conforming to the values of society, they usually live in and on society. A lot of nonsense is talked about this tendency. Bohemians may be parasites, but that is true of many other people. On the other hand, they don't hurt anyone except themselves, which is not true of many other people. The best thing that can be said about them is that they can do some good by enjoying themselves and challenging received values in an ostentatious but harmless way. The worst thing that can be said about them is that they cannot really change society and may divert energy from trying to do this, which for most anarchists is the whole point of anarchism.

A more consistent and constructive way of dropping out of society is to leave it and set up a new self-sufficient community. This has at times been a widespread phenomenon, among religious enthusiasts during the Middle Ages, for instance, and among many kinds of people more recently, especially in North America. Anarchists have been affected by this tendency in the past but not much nowadays; like other left-wing groups, they are more likely to set up their own informal community, based on a network of people living and working together within society, than to secede from society. This may be thought of as the nucleus of a new form of society growing inside the old forms, or else as a viable form of refuge from the demands of authority which is not too extreme for ordinary people.

Another form of action which is based on pessimistic view of the prospects for anarchism is *permanent protest*. According to this view, there is no hope of changing society, of destroying the state system and of putting anarchism into practice. What is important is not the future, the strict adherence to a fixed ideal and the careful elaboration of a beautiful utopia but the present, the belated recognition of a bitter reality and the constant resistance to an ugly situation. Permanent protest is the theory of many former anarchists who have not given up their beliefs but no longer hope for success. It is also the practice of many active anarchists who keep their beliefs intact and carry on as if they still hoped for success but who know—consciously or unconsciously—that they will never see it. What most anarchists have been involved in during the last century may be described as permanent protest when it is looked at with hindsight; but it is just as dogmatic to say that things will never change as to say that things are bound to change, and no one call tell when protest might become effective and the present might suddenly turn into the future. The real distinction is that permanent protest is thought of as a rearguard action in a hopeless cause, while most anarchist activity is thought of as the action of a vanguard or at least of scouts in a struggle which we may not win and which may never end but which is still worth fighting.

The best tactics in this struggle are all those which are consistent with the general strategy of the war for freedom and equality, from guerrilla skirmishes in one's private life to set battles in major social campaigns. Anarchists are almost always in a small minority, so they have little choice of battlefield but have to fight wherever the action is.

In general, the most successful occasions have been those when anarchist agitation has led to anarchist participation in wider left-wing movements—especially in the labour movement, but also in anti-militarist or even pacifist movement in countries preparing for or fighting in wars, anticlerical and humanist movements in religious countries, movements for national or colonial liberation, for racial or sexual equality, for legal or penal reform, or for civil liberties in general.

Such participation inevitably means alliance with non-anarchist groups and some compromise of anarchist principles, and anarchists who become deeply involved in such action are always in danger of abandoning anarchism altogether. On the other hand, refusal to take such a risk generally means sterility and sectarianism, and the anarchist movement has tended to be influential only when it has accepted a full part. The particular anarchist contribution to such occasions is twofold—to emphasise the goal of libertarian society, and to insist on libertarian methods of achieving it. This in in fact a single contribution, for the most important point we can make is not just that the end does not justify the means, but that the means determines the end—that means *are* ends in most cases. We can be sure of our own actions but not of the consequences.

In the old days the greatest opportunities for really substantial movement towards anarchism were in militant syndicalist episodes in France, Spain, Italy, Latin, America, the United States and Russia, and above all in revolutionary movements in France, Mexico, China, Russia and Spain. More recently such opportunities have arisen not so much in the violent and authoritarian revolutions of Asia, Africa and South America as in such non-sectarian movements as the Committee of 100 in Britain, the 22 March Movement in France, the SDS in West Germany, the Provos and Kabouters in the Netherlands, the Zengakuren in Japan and the various movements for civil rights, resistance to conscription, student power, women's liberation, squatters, and the Green movement in many parts of the West. But the most stirring episodes of all have been the more radical insurrectionary upheavals such as those of Hungary in 1956, France and Czechoslovakia in 1968, Portugal in 1974, Poland in 1980—and Britain when?

■ About the Authors

Nicolas Walter (1934–2000) was one of the best-known and most widely read anarchist writers of the last half century. His *About Anarchism* has been translated into many languages, including Russian, Greek, Turkish, Chinese and Japanese. His immense output was otherwise overwhelmingly journalism for the libertarian press. An edited collection of his writings was published by PM Press in 2011 as *Damned Fools in Utopia: And Other Writings on Anarchism and War Resistance*.

Natasha Walter is a British feminist writer and human rights activist. She is the author of a novel, *A Quiet Life*, and two works of feminist non-fiction, *Living Dolls: The Return of Sexism* and *The New Feminism*. She is also the founder of the charity Women for Refugee Women.

David Goodway is a British social and cultural historian who for thirty years has written principally on anarchism and libertarian socialism. He is the author of *Anarchist Seeds beneath the Snow: Left-Libertarian Thought and British Writers from William Morris to Colin Ward* and editor of *For Anarchism*, *Herbert Read Reassessed*, *The Letters of John Cowper Powys and Emma Goldman*, and collections of the writings of Alex Comfort, Herbert Read, Maurice Brinton and Nicolas Walter.

ABOUT PM PRESS

PM Press was founded at the end of 2007 by a small collection of folks with decades of publishing, media, and organizing experience. PM Press co-conspirators have published and distributed hundreds of books, pamphlets, CDs, and DVDs. Members of PM have founded enduring book fairs, spearheaded victorious tenant organizing campaigns, and worked closely with bookstores, academic conferences, and even rock bands to deliver political and challenging ideas to all walks of life. We're old enough to know what we're doing and young enough to know what's at stake.

We seek to create radical and stimulating fiction and nonfiction books, pamphlets, T-shirts, visual and audio materials to entertain, educate, and inspire you. We aim to distribute these through every available channel with every available technology—whether that means you are seeing anarchist classics at our bookfair stalls, reading our latest vegan cookbook at the café, downloading geeky fiction e-books, or digging new music and timely videos from our website.

PM Press is always on the lookout for talented and skilled volunteers, artists, activists, and writers to work with. If you have a great idea for a project or can contribute in some way, please get in touch.

PM Press
PO Box 23912
Oakland, CA 94623
www.pmpress.org

PM Press in Europe
europe@pmpress.org
www.pmpress.org.uk

FRIENDS OF PM PRESS

These are indisputably momentous times—the financial system is melting down globally and the Empire is stumbling. Now more than ever there is a vital need for radical ideas.

In the years since its founding—and on a mere shoestring—PM Press has risen to the formidable challenge of publishing and distributing knowledge and entertainment for the struggles ahead. With over 300 releases to date, we have published an impressive and stimulating array of literature, art, music, politics, and culture. Using every available medium, we've succeeded in connecting those hungry for ideas and information to those putting them into practice.

Friends of PM allows you to directly help impact, amplify, and revitalize the discourse and actions of radical writers, filmmakers, and artists. It provides us with a stable foundation from which we can build upon our early successes and provides a much-needed subsidy for the materials that can't necessarily pay their own way. You can help make that happen—and receive every new title automatically delivered to your door once a month—by joining as a Friend of PM Press. And, we'll throw in a free T-shirt when you sign up.

Here are your options:

- **$30 a month** Get all books and pamphlets plus 50% discount on all webstore purchases

- **$40 a month** Get all PM Press releases (including CDs and DVDs) plus 50% discount on all webstore purchases

- **$100 a month** Superstar—Everything plus PM merchandise, free downloads, and 50% discount on all webstore purchases

For those who can't afford $30 or more a month, we have **Sustainer Rates** at $15, $10 and $5. Sustainers get a free PM Press T-shirt and a 50% discount on all purchases from our website.

Your Visa or Mastercard will be billed once a month, until you tell us to stop. Or until our efforts succeed in bringing the revolution around. Or the financial meltdown of Capital makes plastic redundant. Whichever comes first.

FREEDOM

ABOUT FREEDOM PRESS

The oldest anarchist publishing house in the English-speaking world, Freedom Press was founded in London by a group of volunteers including Charlotte Wilson and Peter Kropotkin in 1886.

The Press has repeatedly been the target of state repression, from crackdowns in the 1890s to raids during World War I and most famously, at the end of World War II. The 1945 free speech case, which saw four editors of its journal *War Commentary* arrested for causing "disaffection in the armed forces," prompted support from many famous names including Herbert Read, George Orwell, Benjamin Britten, and E.M. Forster. Three were jailed.

Despite this and many other threats, from fascists to organised crime, for over a century Freedom has regularly published works on the philosophy and activities of anarchists, and produced its *Freedom Newspaper* for the best part of a century. Freedom now maintains an anarchist-focused news site, www.freedomnews.org.uk, and publishes a biannual free journal.

Freedom runs Britain's largest anarchist bookshop at its home of more than 50 years in Whitechapel, in the heart of London. The upper floors of the Freedom building are home to a number of anarchist organisations, and the venue regularly hosts talks, meetings, and events for the wider movement.

About the Freedom Press Library Series

Freedom Press has partnered with PM Press to republish titles from Freedom's back catalogue, bringing important works back into circulation with new introductions and additional commentary. *About Anarchism* is part of this series.

Freedom Press
84b Whitechapel High St
London, E1 7QX

www.freedompress.org.uk
www.freedomnews.org.uk

Damned Fools in Utopia: And Other Writings on Anarchism and War Resistance

Nicolas Walter
Edited by David Goodway

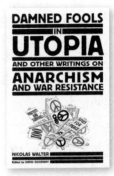

ISBN: 978-1-60486-222-5
$22.95   304 pages

Nicolas Walter was the son of the neurologist W. Grey Walter, and both his grandfathers had known Peter Kropotkin and Edward Carpenter. However, it was the twin jolts of Suez and the Hungarian Revolution while still a student, followed by participation in the resulting New Left and nuclear disarmament movement, that led him to anarchism himself. His personal history is recounted in two autobiographical pieces in this collection as well as the editor's introduction.

During the 1960s he was a militant in the British nuclear disarmament movement—especially its direct-action wing, the Committee of 100—he was one of the Spies for Peace (who revealed the State's preparations for the governance of Britain after a nuclear war), he was close to the innovative Solidarity Group and was a participant in the homelessness agitation. Concurrently with his impressive activism he was analyzing acutely and lucidly the history, practice and theory of these intertwined movements; and it is such writings—including 'Non-violent Resistance' and 'The Spies for Peace and After'—that form the core of this book. But there are also memorable pieces on various libertarians, including the writers George Orwell, Herbert Read and Alan Sillitoe, the publisher C.W. Daniel and the maverick Guy A. Aldred. 'The Right to be Wrong' is a notable polemic against laws limiting the freedom of expression. Other than anarchism, the passion of Walter's intellectual life was the dual cause of atheism and rationalism; and the selection concludes appropriately with a fine essay on 'Anarchism and Religion' and his moving reflections, 'Facing Death'.

Nicolas Walter scorned the pomp and frequent ignorance of the powerful and detested the obfuscatory prose and intellectual limitations of academia. He himself wrote straightforwardly and always accessibly, almost exclusively for the anarchist and freethought movements. The items collected in this volume display him at his considerable best.

"[Nicolas Walter was] one of the most interesting left intellectuals of the second half of the twentieth century in Britain."
—Professor Richard Taylor, University of Cambridge

Anarchist Seeds beneath the Snow: Left-Libertarian Thought and British Writers from William Morris to Colin Ward

David Goodway

ISBN: 978-1-60486-221-8
$24.95   420 pages

From William Morris to Oscar Wilde to George Orwell, left-libertarian thought has long been an important but neglected part of British cultural and political history. In *Anarchist Seeds beneath the Snow*, David Goodway seeks to recover and revitalize that indigenous anarchist tradition. This book succeeds as simultaneously a cultural history of left-libertarian thought in Britain and a demonstration of the applicability of that history to current politics. Goodway argues that a recovered anarchist tradition could—and should—be a touchstone for contemporary political radicals. Moving seamlessly from Aldous Huxley and Colin Ward to the war in Iraq, this challenging volume will energize leftist movements throughout the world.

"*Anarchist Seeds beneath the Snow is an impressive achievement for its rigorous scholarship across a wide range of sources, for collating this diverse material in a cogent and systematic narrative-cum-argument, and for elucidating it with clarity and flair . . . It is a book that needed to be written and now deserves to be read.*"
—*Journal of William Morris Studies*

"*Goodway outlines with admirable clarity the many variations in anarchist thought. By extending outwards to left-libertarians he takes on even greater diversity.*"
—Sheila Rowbotham, *Red Pepper*

"*A splendid survey of 'left-libertarian thought' in this country, it has given me hours of delight and interest. Though it is very learned, it isn't dry. Goodway's friends in the awkward squad (especially William Blake) are both stimulating and comforting companions in today's political climate.*"
—A.N. Wilson, *Daily Telegraph*

Lessons of the Spanish Revolution: 1936–1939

Vernon Richards with an
Introduction by David Goodway

ISBN: 978-1-62963-647-4
$21.95   272 pages

It was the revolutionary movement in
Spain which took up Franco's challenge in
July 1936, not as supporters of the Popular
Front Government but in the name of the Social Revolution, and this
book soberly examines the many ways in which Spain's revolutionary
movement contributed to its own defeat.

Was it too weak to carry through the Revolution? To what extent was
the purchase of arms and raw materials from outside sources dependent
upon the appearance of a constitutional government inside Republican
Spain? What chances had an improvised army of guerrillas against a
trained fighting force? These were some of the practical problems facing
the revolutionary movement and its leaders. But in seeking to solve
these problems, the anarchists and revolutionary syndicalists were also
confronted with other questions which were fundamental to the whole
theoretical and moral bases of their organisation. Could they collaborate
with political parties and reformist unions? Given the circumstances,
was one form of government to be supported against another? Should
the revolutionary impetus of the first days of resistance be halted in
the interests of the armed struggle against Franco or be allowed to
develop as far as the workers were able and prepared to take it? Was the
situation such that the social revolution could triumph and, if not, what
was to be the role of the revolutionary workers?

Originally written as a series of weekly articles in the 1950s and
expanded, republished, and translated into many languages over the
years, Vernon Richards's analysis remains essential reading for all those
interested in revolutionary praxis.

*"The revolution that accompanied the outbreak of the Spanish Civil War was
a high point in the history of working-class creativity, internationalism and
self-activity. If it is to be a resource for present and future struggles, we must
assess the strengths and weaknesses of the movement that propelled it. In
this regard, the early endeavours of Vernon Richards remain indispensable."*
—Danny Evans, author of *Revolution and the State: Anarchism in the
Spanish Civil War, 1936–1939*

Anarchy in Action

Colin Ward

ISBN: 978-1-62963-238-4
$15.95   192 pages

The argument of this book is that an anarchist
society, a society which organizes itself
without authority, is always in existence,
like a seed beneath the snow, buried under
the weight of the state and its bureaucracy,
capitalism and its waste, privilege and its
injustices, nationalism and its suicidal loyalties, religious differences and
their superstitious separatism.

Anarchist ideas are so much at variance with ordinary political
assumptions and the solutions anarchists offer so remote, that all too
often people find it hard to take anarchism seriously. This classic text is
an attempt to bridge the gap between the present reality and anarchist
aspirations, "between what is and what, according to the anarchists,
might be."

Through a wide-ranging analysis—drawing on examples from education,
urban planning, welfare, housing, the environment, the workplace, and
the family, to name but a few—Colin Ward demonstrates that the
roots of anarchist practice are not so alien or quixotic as they might at
first seem but lie precisely in the ways that people have always tended
to organize themselves when left alone to do so. The result is both
an accessible introduction for those new to anarchism and pause for
thought for those who are too quick to dismiss it.

For more than thirty years, in over thirty books, Colin Ward patiently
explained anarchist solutions to everything from vandalism to climate
change—and celebrated unofficial uses of the landscape as commons,
from holiday camps to squatter communities. Ward was an anarchist
journalist and editor for almost sixty years, most famously editing the
journal *Anarchy*. He was also a columnist for *New Statesman*, *New Society*,
Freedom, and *Town and Country Planning*.

"It is difficult to match the empirical strength, the lucidity of prose, and the
integration of theory and practical insight in the magnificent body of work
produced by the veteran anarchist Colin Ward."
—*Prospect*

The Slow Burning Fuse: The Lost History of the British Anarchists

John Quail with an Afterword by Constance Bantman and biographical sketches by Nick Heath

ISBN: 978-1-62963-582-8
$27.95   416 pages

In the accounts of the radical movements that have shaped our history, anarchism has received a raw deal. Its visions and aims have been distorted and misunderstood, its achievements forgotten. The British anarchist movement during the years 1880–1930, while borrowing from Europe, was self-actuated and independent, with a vibrant tale all its own.

In *The Slow Burning Fuse*, John Quail shows a history largely obscured and rewritten following 1919 and the triumph of Leninist communism. The time has arrived to resurrect the works of the early anarchist clubs, their unsung heroes, tumultuous political activities, and searing manifestos so that a truer image of radical dissent and history can be formed. Quail's story of the anarchists is one of utopias created in imagination and half-realised in practice, of individual fights and movements for freedom and self-expression—a story still being written today.

"The Slow Burning Fuse *is a meticulous, accessible and riveting account of the British anarchist movement. John Quail introduces us to the anarchists of the Socialist League, explores the early history of the Freedom group, describes the murky world of police spies and agents provocateurs, and shows how small groups of anarchists in London and Sheffield animated working-class movements at the turn of the twentieth century. Quail's rich history is also an unflinching reflection on anarchist organising. Examining the personal feuds that plagued the movement and the political disagreements generated by the incidence of violence in France, Quail shows how internal divisions exacerbated the problems created by systematic police repression. Anarchist utopian aspirations are easily romanticised or mocked. Quail avoids both and instead invites us to weigh up the value of spectacular actions and consider the effectiveness of strategic initiatives. The result is a passionate but sober defence of anarchist politics and movement building.*"
—Ruth Kinna, author of *Kropotkin: Reviewing the Classical Anarchist Tradition*

What Is Anarchism?: An Introduction
Second Edition

Donald Rooum,
edited by Vernon Richards
with a foreword by Andrej Grubačić

ISBN: 978-1-62963-146-2
$14.95   160 pages

Anarchists believe that the point of society
is to widen the choices of individuals. Anarchism is opposed to states,
armies, slavery, the wages system, the landlord system, prisons,
capitalism, bureaucracy, meritocracy, theocracy, revolutionary
governments, patriarchy, matriarchy, monarchy, oligarchy, and every
other kind of coercive institution. In other words, anarchism opposes
government in all its forms.

Enlarged and updated for a modern audience, *What Is Anarchism?*
has the making of a standard reference book. As an introduction to
the development of anarchist thought, it will be useful not only to
propagandists and proselytizers of anarchism but also to teachers and
students of political theory, philosophy, sociology, history, and to all who
want to uncover the basic core of anarchism.

This useful compendium, compiled and edited by the late Vernon
Richards of Freedom Press, with additional selections by Donald Rooum,
includes extracts from the work of Errico Malatesta, Peter Kropotkin,
Max Stirner, Emma Goldman, Charlotte Wilson, Michael Bakunin, Rudolf
Rocker, Alexander Berkman, Colin Ward, Albert Meltzer, and many
others.

Author and Wildcat cartoonist Donald Rooum gives context to the
selections with introductions looking at "What Anarchists Believe,"
"How Anarchists Differ," and "What Anarchists Do" and provides helpful
and humorous illustrations throughout the book.

"*What Is Anarchism? is a classic. It brings together a marvellous selection
of inspiring texts with a clear, comprehensive introduction—now updated—
to provide a brilliant account of the cares, concerns and commitments that
animate anarchist politics and activities of British anarchists since 1945.*"
—Ruth Kinna, author of *Anarchism: A Beginner's Guide*